Fit for Riding

Richard Meade

General Editor   Peter Verney
Medical Adviser   Dr Alan Maryon-Davis
MB, Bchir, MSc, MRCP, MFCM
Medical Officer
Health Education Council

B T Batsford Ltd · London

(© Gerald Broadhead)

© Richard Meade, Alan Maryon-Davis 1984
First published 1984

All rights reserved. No part of this publication
may be reproduced, in any form or by any means,
without permission from the Publisher

ISBN 0 7134 4223 9

Typeset by Tek-Art Ltd, Kent
and printed in Great Britain by
R J Acford
Chichester, Sussex
for the publishers
B.T. Batsford Ltd.
4 Fitzhardinge Street
London W1H 0AH

Contents

Foreword 4

Section 1 General Fitness 5

The Fitness Ethic – Fit for Sport? – Fitness Testing – Fitness Tests – The Elements of Fitness – Fitness Exercises – Exercise Sessions – Suppleness Exercises – Strength Exercises – Stamina Exercises – Circuit Training – Warming up – Warming down – Weight and Fitness

Section 2 Fit for Riding 31

Introduction – The Rider: General Fitness Requirements; The Riding Position; Aids; Paces; Levels of Riding Fitness; The Fitness Needs of Riding; Exercise Circuits; Mental Attitude; Avoiding Injury; Clothing; Tack – The Horse; Bringing a Horse to Peak fitness; After-exercise Care; Keeping a Horse Fit and Healthy; Some Important Conditions; Preventative Medecine

Section 3 Ailments and Injuries 55

Introduction – Specific Injuries Associated with Riding – General Ailments and Conditions – First Aid

Index 73

Foreword

If there is one thing certain in this transient world it is that as our working days get shorter, and sometimes fewer in face of technological advance, we shall be 'burdened' by more and more leisure time. Some of us will occupy ourselves in sedentary occupations, but many more will prefer to take more and regular exercise — and this will often mean *devoting greater time and intensity to sport.*

These books are not written with the beginner in mind — although he or she will find much of value in these pages — but they are rather designed for the enthusiastic amateur; the committed sportsman or sportswoman, someone who has tasted, experienced and enjoyed their sport and who wishes to improve their performance and consequently gain greater enjoyment from their sport.

The twin pillars of improvement in any occupation are experience and skill. Experience can only come with time and a long association with the sport, but skill in any sport is dependent on, and in many cases the product of, fitness. A general degree of fitness — physical and mental — is required in the first place to act as foundation for the subsequent developed and specialised fitness which is needed by the enthusiast for his or her chosen sport. It is the purpose of this series of books, written by acknowledged experts of great experience, to help achieve this specific fitness.

Section I of this book is devoted to the attainment of a general fitness level, albeit orientated towards sports fitness. Section II concentrates on the specific needs and related aspects — equipment, training, competition advice, etc. — of riding, and how to attain fitness in riding. Section III deals with the medical aspects of the sport — the injuries and conditions associated with riding and, finally, some First Aid principles, aimed primarily at emergencies which might occur on the course or field, but which will be of use to anyone under any circumstances.

SECTION 1
General Fitness

The Fitness Ethic

One of the most significant trends in everyday living over the past thirty years has been a growing interest in fitness. Books on general fitness abound, and most incorporate an analysis of the need for fitness, the effect of fitness on the human body and the beneficial effect when that body is fit. Although this series is designed with specific sports in mind, there is no doubt that a general degree of fitness is of inestimable value to the sportsman or sportwoman, especially as more and more people are coming into sport at a later age.

The doctors declare that there is a close link between physical fitness and mental alertness, and that a fit person, taking regular exercise, is better able to face the pace and rigours, and the emotional and physical stresses of day-to-day living. He is also more likely to sleep well and feel well. More particularly, a fit body is an efficient body.

In addition, although fitness is not a passport to health, it does make you less liable to sickness and more able to effect a speedy recovery from illness. Of great value in the field of sport is the fact that a fit person tires less easily than someone who is not, and injury in sport is often directly caused by fatigue.

The doctors will also tell you that the fit have stronger hearts, and regular exercise reduces the risk of heart disease; moreover, that lack of exercise is a major cause of heart disease, and that, if you do have a heart attack, you will have a better chance of surviving it if you are fit.

For those participating in sport, fitness gives you confidence that you won't crack up halfway, makes muscle fatigue, pulls and other injuries less likely, and gives you a competitive edge.

Fit for Sport?

Most people are fit enough for most sports and games played at a gentle pace. However, there is a basic assumption behind this series that the reader is proposing to play his sport more regularly and at a greater intensity than hitherto – in short, the committed sportsman. So certain medical warnings are necessary, and a medical check-up is advisable beforehand.

This is particularly important for anyone over 35, especially if taking up strenuous sport for the first time or after a lay-off, or for those with a history of injury or who have suffered a disability or condition which has hindered or prevented them taking regular exercise.

It is important also for those who have or have recently had a heart condition or high blood pressure, asthma or other respiratory problems, arthritis or joint trouble, especially in the back or legs.

Above all, if *you* have any doubt about the effect of regular strenuous exercise on your health, seek medical advice.

Fitness Tests

With a clean bill of medical health, or if you do not feel that a medical check-up is necessary, the next stage is to discover how fit you are.

The fitness tests described on the following pages were devised many years ago and are used as a way of finding out *progressive* levels of fitness. The essence of these tests is that if you cannot perform them without undue effort – this means without breathlessness (and the truest measure of that is whether or not you can carry out a normal conversation) you should not proceed to the next test.

For most people these tests are a formality. The tests themselves are simple, painless and speedy. For the young and healthy they hardly arouse so much as a gentle sweat; but for others – and this series of books is aimed at a broad spectrum of ages and fitness levels – some of the tests may cause severe breathlessness and discomfort. If at any time you do feel discomfort *stop*, and consult medical opinion. And, if you cannot proceed beyond a certain test, it means that your stamina is wanting and you should undertake a conditioning programme.

Fitness Test

The fitness tests listed below are in four stages of increasing difficulty. In addition, a parallel test for pulse rate is shown which specifies more exactly the relative state of your fitness. For anyone regularly engaged in sport these tests are very basic indeed, but for those who are beginning or who have been inactive for some time, they will provide a useful assessment. It is important that you should be completely healthy when carrying out these tests. If you have a cold, cough or other ailment, wait until it has subsided.

Fitness Test 1: Stairs

Walk up and down a flight of 10-15 stairs three times. (*If at any time during this exercise you feel at all uncomfortable – stop.*) At the end you should be hardly breathless and be able to carry on a normal conversation without puffing. If this is the case, proceed to fitness test 2.

Fitness Test 2: Jogging on the Spot

Making sure that you lift your feet a good 20 cm (8 in.) off the floor, run on the spot/jog on the spot for *three minutes*. (*If at any time during this exercise you feel at all uncomfortable – stop.*) Once again at the end you should be able to carry on a normal conversation. If this is the case, proceed to fitness test 3.

Fitness Test 3: Step-ups

Take a strong chair (the *second* step of the stairs used in the first test will do) – the important thing is that the rise should be not less than 35 cm (14 in.) – and step up and down (right leg up, then left leg to join it so you are standing on the chair, then left leg down, followed by right leg down, etc.). Do this briskly for *three minutes* (*two minutes* if aged over 45). (*If at any time during this exercise you feel at all uncomfortable – stop.*) You should be able to carry on a normal conversation after this test. If so, proceed to fitness test 4.

Fitness Test 4: Measured Run

Mark out a measured 1.6 km (1 mile) and then gently jog the distance. (*If at any time during this test you feel at all uncomfortable – stop.*) At the end you should be mildly breathless and your times should be as follows:

Under 45 *Men*: 10 minutes
            Women: 12 minutes
Over 45   add one minute for each span of five
            years

If you are slower than these times you will need to undertake further stamina-improving exercises. Otherwise, when you can perform this test without discomfort or distress, you should be fit enough to start gaining fitness for your chosen sport.

Pulse Rate Test

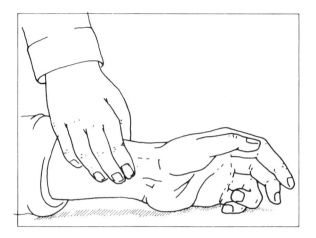

To take the pulse, first place your watch, with an easily seen second hand, where you can observe it. Then, using a pile of large books, a step or stout box – about 20 cm (8 in.) high – step up and down briskly for *three minutes*. (*If at any time you feel at all uncomfortable – stop.*) Rest for *one minute* and take your pulse for one minute. To do this, place three fingers of the right hand on the left wrist some 3 cm (1 ½ in.) below the mound of the thumb (*see illustration*). You should then be able to feel your pulse and count the beats. Check your rating with the table below. (The lower the pulse rate, generally the fitter you are.)

	Men	Women
Excellent	below 68	below 76
Good	68-79	76-85
Average	80-89	86-94
Below average	90-99	95-109
Very poor	100+	110+

If your score is *average* or better, you should be fit enough to start gaining fitness for your chosen sport. If it is *below average* or worse, you should undertake some further stamina-building programme.

The Elements of Fitness

There are three main elements of fitness:

suppleness
strength
stamina

and all three need to be worked on to attain general fitness. In addition, in some sports *muscle endurance*, *speed* and *agility* can also be important. Where applicable, exercises for these will be found in Section II.

Suppleness
(also called flexibility, or mobility)

Suppleness is the degree of movement in the joints and muscles of the body (this includes the neck, back and limbs). A gradual stiffening of the joints is a characteristic of the ageing process, and also occurs through disuse. When this happens, people are far more susceptible to strains and sprains. General suppleness is more important for some sports than others, but specific suppleness is needed in most sports, and suppleness exercises are designed to help develop the maximum range of the joints, limber up the whole body, and reduce the risk of injury.

Strength

Strength broadly means muscle power. And strength can be improved in two ways, through *isometrics* or *dynamics* (also known as isotonics).

Isometrics

Isometrics are essentially static exercises against resistance, and are intended specifically for building up muscle bulk. As such they are much used in body building, or in restoring wasted muscle after injury. They involve little or no movement and, as a result, cannot be used as stamina-improving exercises. Further, they could be dangerous for those over 35 or with high blood pressure.

Dynamics

Dynamics are exercises which do involve movement. In these, the resistance gives way and this has the effect of stretching the muscles. In addition, repetitive exercises have a strengthening effect – through alternately shortening and lengthening the muscles – and, if continued for a sufficient length of time, can also improve stamina (*see below*). Dynamics are in greater general use and have far greater application in sports fitness. Most dynamic exercises take the form of rhythmic activity, e.g. jogging, swimming, skipping.

Stamina
(also called heart and lung endurance or, sometimes, aerobics)

Stamina is essentially staying power – the ability to keep going without undue breathlessness. The muscles of the body are kept fuelled with oxygen carried in the blood stream (their waste products are also borne away in the blood stream). During strenuous exercise the muscles use oxygen at a very rapid rate, if this is not replaced quickly enough the muscles cease to function, and this is the essence of fatigue. Furthermore, the inefficient removal of waste products adds to muscle fatigue and painful exhaustion takes over. In sport, a tired person obviously cannot perform to the best of his or her ability and is also susceptible to injury. Stamina-building exercises aim to increase the efficiency of the heart and the muscles, and improve the circulation of the blood, thus rendering fatigue less likely.

Balanced Fitness

The aim of these exercises is to achieve a *balanced fitness* – extra suppleness keeping pace with improved stamina; strength married with greater flexibility – in short a programme which pays attention to all three components of fitness and exercises all the important parts of the body properly. Circuit training is the most popular way of combining these exercises, and this is discussed in more detail at the end of this section.

How you choose to regulate your exercise is up to you, for training is a matter of personal discretion and individual preference, provided that certain guidelines are adhered to and the regime is gradual and progressive.

Exercise Sessions

It is usually considered that it is necessary to carry out three sessions a week to maintain reasonable standards of fitness. Each session should last about 30 minutes in the following proportion:

20 minutes warm-up and stamina building
10 minutes split between suppleness (*two to three minutes*) and strength (*seven to eight minutes*).

Exercises should be enjoyable. If you lose motivation, *stop*, for the odds are that you will not be doing the exercises correctly to get maximum benefit from them and, if you allow your concentration to lapse, you could injure yourself.

Never exercise to the point of distress or complete breathlessness, on the other hand don't be afraid to break into a sweat. The golden rules of exercise are:
exercise conscientiously;
never to the point of distress;
never to the point of complete breathlessness;
exercise regularly;
exercise gradually, but progressively.

Suppleness Exercises

When doing these exercises it is important to stretch gradually. Push until it feels slightly uncomfortable. Hold for a second or two, then relax and repeat. For rolling exercises, rotate the part on as wide an arc as possible so that you feel you have moved over the full range.

In general, suppleness exercise sessions work systematically through all parts of the body – neck, shoulders, arms, chest, trunk, hips and legs. Repeat movements five to ten times with progressively more effort.

Spine and Hips

1 *Side Bends*

(Standing erect, with feet comfortably apart, hands at sides.)

Bend trunk to the left and at same time slide

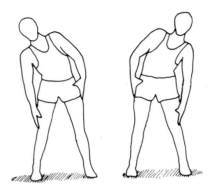

hands down the calf as far as possible keeping the back straight. Return to the upright position. Then repeat on the other side.

Starting repetitions: 6 each side

2 *Trunks Twists*

(Standing erect, with feet comfortably apart, hands on hips.)

Twist the trunk alternately from side to side, keeping the back as straight as possible.

Starting repetitions: 6 each side

Spine, Hips and Hamstrings

3 *Alternate Toe Touches*

(Standing erect, with feet comfortably apart, arms raised.)

Bend down and touch the opposite toe – e.g. right hand to left toe. Then return to the upright

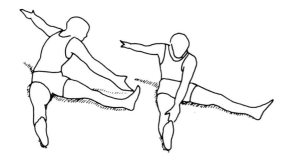

position and touch the right toe with the left hand, and so on. It is important to return to the upright position with the back straight.

If you cannot touch the toes, reach down as far as is comfortable. As you become more supple you will find that you can reach down further and further.

Variation: carry out the exercise sitting down.
Starting repetitions: 6 each side

4 *Neck Rolls*

(Standing, or sitting erect [this is an exercise which can be done at any time] with feet comfortably apart, hands on hips.)

Drop chin to the chest and then slowly roll the head round reaching as far over the shoulders as is comfortable. Repeat clockwise and anti-clockwise.
Starting repetitions: 10

Shoulders

5 *Shoulder Shrugs*

(Standing erect, with feet comfortably apart, hands hanging loosely at the sides.)

Raise shoulders as high as you can shrug and then pull them down as far as you can.
Starting repetitions: 15

6 *Wing Stretchers*

(Standing erect, with feet comfortably apart, arms parallel with ground and folded as in the drawing.)

Force the elbows back as far as they will comfortably go. Count two, and relax. The body should remain upright and the head erect.
Starting repetitions: 10

Arms and Upper Body

7 Arm Circles

(Standing erect, with feet comfortably apart, arms forward at shoulder height as in the drawing.)

Bring the arms upwards brushing the ears, then around to the starting position. Flex the wrists and fingers while doing so.

Variation: hold the arms out sideways and describe small circling movements which

gradually get larger until the full swing is achieved. Practise both forwards and backwards.
Starting repetitions: 6

8 Arm Flings

(Standing, erect, with feet comfortably apart, arms held as in exercise 6, but with fingertips touching.)

Fling first the left arm out as far as it will comfortably go (keep it parallel to the ground, there is a tendency to let it droop.) Then return to the central position and repeat with the right arm. Keep the body and head erect throughout the exercise.
Starting repetitions: 10

Wrists

9 Wrist Shakes

(Standing [or sitting] erect.)

Hold out arms. Let the hands droop and then shake the wrists and hands up, down and sideways, keeping the forearm still throughout.
Starting repetitions: 15 seconds

Abdomen, Thighs and Calves

10 *The Reach*

(Standing erect, with feet comfortably apart, hands hanging loosely at the sides.)
Breathe in deeply and slowly bend backwards, at same time reach upwards with fingers outstretched. Breathe out. Hold position for 5

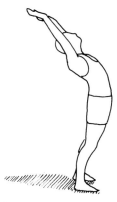

seconds before returning to the upright position. Breathe in deeply, then repeat.
Starting repetitions: 6

11 *The Lunge*

(Standing erect, with feet comfortably apart, and hands on hips.)
Stride sideways with the right leg pivoting the feet as in the drawing. Adopt a lunging position as in fencing. Keep pushing the right leg back, and keeping it straight at the same time, while forcing the body towards the floor. Hold for a count of 5, relax and repeat with the other leg. Keep the back straight throughout and the forward leg vertical.
Starting repetitions: 4 each side

12 *Hurdles*

(Sitting on the floor, as in the drawing, with right leg outstretched and left leg bent at right angles.)
Place hands on top of right leg and reach down towards the foot, bending the body, neck and head as close to the leg as possible (at first it will

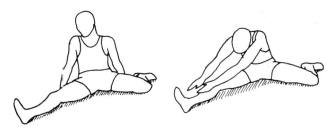

not be possible to reach very far down the extended leg, but as suppleness increases this will improve). Do not overstretch or bounce. Apply a steady pressure only, then relax. Repeat on other side.
Starting repetitions: 5 each leg

Upper Legs

13 *Leg Swings*

(Standing erect, with feet comfortably apart, arms outstretched. For balance hold on to a chair, table or door handle.)

Swing the outer leg backwards and forwards as far as you can comfortably go. Relax and repeat on the other side.
Starting repetitions: 6 each side

14 *Knee Pulls*

(Lying flat on the ground.)
Pull first one knee, then the other – or both knees – into the chest. Hold for a count of 5, then relax and repeat. Either keep the head on the floor or bring it forward to the knee.

Variation: stand erect and lift one knee as high as you can and clasp it to the chest. Hold for a count of 5, then relax and repeat with the other leg.
Starting repetitions: 4 each leg

Lower Legs

15 *Calf Stretches*

(Standing at arm's length away from a wall, with the feet together and hands together.)
Lean forward, bending the arms and keeping the feet flat on the floor. Straighten and relax. Repeat.
Variation: this exercise can also be used to strengthen the fingers by pushing the body upright using the fingers rather than the hands.
Starting repetitions: 15

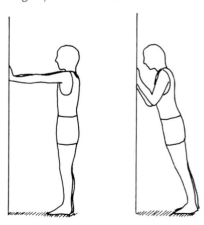

Strength Exercises

These exercises are designed primarily to strengthen muscles and ligaments and, by the use of high repetition, to improve muscle endurance.

Strength exercises work on the 'overload' principle, where repetitions or resistance, or both, are gradually increased.

It is a great mistake to launch oneself into strength exercises without adequate warm-up (*see p.27*), otherwise there is a high risk of pulled muscles, etc.

The exercises below are graded by degree of difficulty

* easy
** difficult
*** very difficult

Do not attempt the most difficult until you think you can manage them comfortably.

Body, Arms and Shoulders

1 *Push-ups (Press-ups)*

Degree of difficulty:
Normal**
With stool***
Modified*

(Lying on the floor face downwards, feet together and hands under the shoulders.)

Push the body off the floor by straightening the arms. Then lower the body to the floor by bending the arms. It is important to keep the back straight.

Variations: try using a stool, as shown in illustrations (b) and (c), for greater strenuousness (*see star gradings*).

The modified push-up is an easier variation (see drawing [d]).

Starting repetitions: 6

17

Arms and Shoulders

2 *Pull-ups*

Degree of difficulty:
Normal***
Modified**

(After finding a strong bar just out of reach of the upstretched arms.)
  Jump up and grasp it, either with palms facing the face or away from it, as shown. Hang for a moment, then slowly pull the body up until the chin is level with the hands. Hold, then relax and repeat. Try to avoid swaying, and keep the feet together.

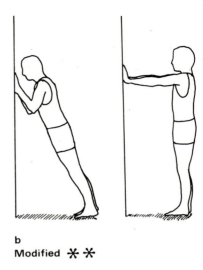

b
Modified ✳✳

a
✳✳✳

The modified pull-up is based on the position of suppleness exercise 15, but with the feet further from the wall, as shown in illustration (b). Push the body upright until the arms are straight, then bend the arms and allow the body to fall forward again. Using the fingers helps strengthen them. Make sure your footing is secure.
  Starting repetitions: 4

3 *Hip Raises*

Degree of difficulty: ✳

(Sitting on the floor, with legs and feet together and hands placed flat on the ground.)
  Raise the body using only the hands, until the arms are straight. Hold for a count of 5, then relax and repeat. The body should be vertical and arms completely straight when raised from the floor.
  Variation: by placing a book/books under the hands the exercise can be made more difficult.
  Starting repetitions: 8

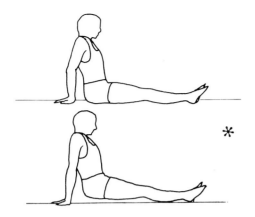

Wrists and Arms

4 *Broomstick Roll*

Degree of difficulty: *

(Standing erect, with feet comfortably apart.)
Take a length of broomstick about 1 in. in diameter and 2 ft long, having tied a length of string to the centre point long enough to be 3-4 in.

from the floor. To this is tied a weight – plastic bag of sand, a brick, a tin can holding water, etc. (start with a light weight and build up). Then, using both hands, palms down, wind the string on to the broomstick.

It is easier to do the exercise with the elbows bent and hands close to the chest, as in the drawing. Then carry out the exercise with the arms straight in front.

When the weight reaches the top, slowly wind it down again.

Starting repetitions: 6

5 *Tennis Ball Squeeze*

Degree of difficulty: *

Taking a tennis ball, two squash balls, or other rubber ball, in the hand, squeeze as hard as you can. Hold for a count of 5 seconds, relax and repeat.

Variation: hold the tennis ball in front of you, with arms straight and fingers of both hands interlocking. Squeeze the ball as hard as you can until you feel the effect in the shoulder muscles. Hold for 5 seconds, then relax and repeat.

Starting repetitions: 6

6 *Fingertip Push-ups*

Degree of difficulty: ***

This is an adaptation of the push-up (strength exercise 1) using the fingers rather than the flat of the hands (see illustration).

Starting repetitions: 4

***

7 Fingertip Hip Raise

Degree of difficulty: **

This is an adaptation of the hip raise (strength exercise 3) using the fingers rather than the flat of the hand.
 Starting repetitions: 6

**

Abdomen

8 Bicycling

Degree of difficulty: **

(Lying on the back as shown in the illustration.)
 Carry out a bicycling movement with the legs. Pull back the knee as far towards the face as comfortable then straighten it fully.
 Starting repetitions: 10 seconds

**

9 Bent-leg Sit-ups

Degree of difficulty:
Normal**
Variation***

(Lying on the back, legs bent and arms to the side with the feet under a low bar – wardrobe, chair or sofa – or with someone holding the ankles.)
 Raise the body *slowly* to a sitting position leaning forward, trying to touch the knees with the head. Then *slowly* return to the sitting position.

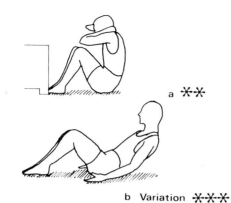

a ✶✶

b Variation ✶✶✶

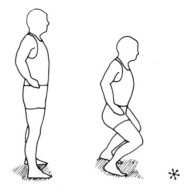

✶

Variation: try a trunk twist at the top of the sit-up. Later, exercise without a foot support, as in illustration (b).

It is wrong to use the hands as a lever to assist or hold the position. Place the hands behind the head to remove temptation.

Starting repetitions: 4

Thighs and Legs

10 *Half Squats*

Degree of difficulty: *

(Standing erect, with feet comfortably apart, hands on hips.)

Rise on the toes and *slowly* sink down, bending the knees until the half-squat position is adopted. Hold for count of 5 seconds, then stand upright again. Relax and repeat.

Keep the body upright, the tendency is to lean forward.

Starting repetitions: 6

11 *Squat Thrusts (Burpees)*

Degree of difficulty: ✶✶

(Start as shown in illustration)

Shoot out the legs behind you into the push-up position, and then bring them forward again. Keep the feet together at all times.

Starting repetitions: 6

✶✶

12 *Sprinters*

Degree of difficulty: **

A variation on squat thrusts (burpees), but using only one leg at a time. Keep the back straight at all times.
  Starting repetitions: 6

**

13 *Paint Can Raises*

Degree of difficulty: *

(Sitting on a chair or bench, with thighs parallel to the ground and lower legs at right angles.)
  Take a paint can, or similar object which can be filled to the extent required to give weight, and hook it on the toe of one foot. Raise the weight *slowly* until the leg is straight, and then *slowly* lower it to the ground again. Repeat, and then change legs.
  It is important to keep the knees together. Grasping the chair will make the exercise easier to start with.
  Starting repetitions: 6

*

14 *Leg Raises*

Degree of difficulty:
Single *
Double **
Side *

(Lying flat on the back, with hands on the floor, palms down.)
  Raise one leg *slowly* about 9 in. then *slowly* lower it again. Relax. Repeat with the other leg.

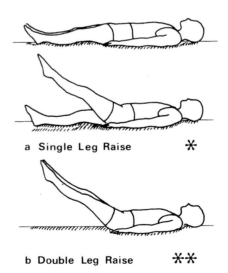

a Single Leg Raise   *

b Double Leg Raise   **

22

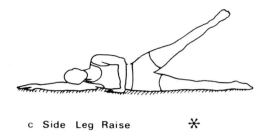

c Side Leg Raise

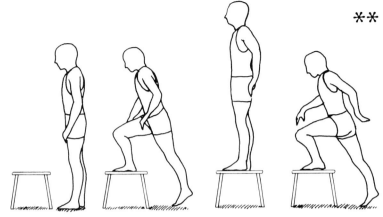

Variations: double leg raises and side leg raises, as illustrated in (b) and (c).

It is important to keep completely flat on the floor, including the head. Using the hands to help lever the legs will make the exercise easier to start with, but should be resisted as soon as possible.

Starting repetitions: 6

15 Step-ups

Degree of difficulty: **

(Standing erect, with hands at the sides facing the chair, stool or pile of large books 12-18 in. high.)

Place the right foot on the stool and, by using only the power of the legs, raise the body until standing on the stool. Step down again *slowly*. Repeat with the left leg. The body should remain upright throughout. There is a tendency to lurch forwards when mounting the stool. At first put the whole foot on the stool, later use only the toes.

Starting repetitions: 6

16 Bench Jumps

Degree of difficulty: **

(Standing alongside a bench, pile of books or bricks.)

Jump with feet together from one side to the other, and back again.

Variations: jump with feet astride, landing on the bench; hop on one leg either onto or over the bench; carry a weight, jumping on the toes rather than the whole foot, etc.

It is important to stand upright, there is a tendency to lurch either forwards or sideways. Carried out at speed, bench jumps are an excellent stamina-building exercise.

Starting repetitions: 6

23

Lower Legs

17 *Shin Strengtheners*

Degree of difficulty: *

This is a variation on paint can raises (strength exercise 13). Instead of raising the whole leg,

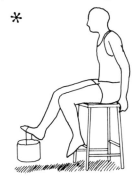

raise only the foot, bending at the heel. It is important to raise and lower slowly. Hold at the high level for a count of 5 seconds, then lower. Repeat, then change the can to the other foot. Holding on to the bench or chair while doing the exercise is a help to start with, but should be resisted later.
Starting repetitions: 4

18 *Calf Raises*

Degree of difficulty: *

(Standing erect with arms at the sides, toes on the edge of a shallow step, or large book.)
    Bring the arms forward and at the same time rise on the toes. Lower *slowly,* relax and repeat.

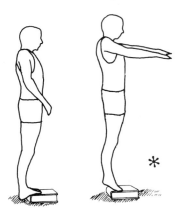

The body should remain upright throughout; there is a tendency to lean forward.
    Variation: instead of rising fully on the toes, rise only halfway, and hold the position for a count of 4-5 seconds.
Starting repetitions: 6

Stamina-building Exercises

As applies for all exercises, those for stamina building should be regular – 20-minute sessions, three times a week is ideal.

Walking

Walking is probably the best way gradually to build up stamina for the unfit, the partially fit, or those who have not been taking regular exercise for some time.

This should not be just a gentle amble, but a purposeful exercise; breathing in deeply and keeping the back straight and the head up, walk briskly, lengthening the stride and the distance gradually.

Jogging

Jogging is probably the most popular form of stamina building. It is also an excellent exercise at the start of a warm-up routine (*see p.28*).

Running/Jogging on the Spot

This is an excellent exercise provided the legs are lifted high enough (30 cm [12 in.]). It is also useful for strengthening the leg muscles, particularly the hamstrings.

Skipping (rope work), bicycling and swimming are all good stamina-building exercises as are certain strength exercises if performed sufficiently vigorously at high repetition. These include:

Push-ups, modified if necessary (*Str. 1*)
Pull-ups, modified if necessary (*Str. 2*)
'Bicycling' (*Str. 8*)
Squat thrusts (Burpees) (*Str. 11*)
Step-ups (*Str. 15*)
Bench Jumps (*Str. 16*)

Build up your repetitions gradually, but make your routine progressive.

Circuit Training

Circuit training is nothing more than a range of exercises (eight to ten is usual) concentrating on different parts of the body. The mix comprises suppleness and strength exercises, so stamina building must be additional to the basic circuit, unless the circuit is done at sufficient intensity to constitute a stamina-building routine in itself. There are a number of criteria in choosing and using a training circuit:

1   The circuit should start with warm-up exercises to tone up the muscles and prevent muscle strain.
2   No two successive exercises should work on the same part of the body, thus giving variety.
3   The training programme must be progressive and comprehensive.

Within these parameters the choice is wide and

entirely personal. Three examples of circuits to help attain general fitness are listed below.

Method

First of all go through the whole circuit to familiarise yourself with the exercises – this is particularly important for the not-so-young and the not-so-fit – making sure that each exercise is carried out properly.

Having absorbed the general requirements of the circuit, you can get down to circuit training proper. Remember, never force yourself, and you should never be more than moderately breathless.

It is useful and interesting to keep a check on progress, so have a clock or watch handy. Start off by doing each circuit three times at your own speed, and then pausing for five minutes before doing another series. Time each series. The point of keeping times is to enable you to judge when you have reached a plateau in your training and the time has come for a variation. Such variation should be *gradual* and *progressive*.

The asset of circuit training is that it is possible to alter the routine in many different ways:

1 By doing the circuit faster.
2 By increasing the number of circuits before pausing.
3 By decreasing the pause time between circuits.
4 By increasing the number of repetitions within the circuit (and if you feel that you need to work on any particular weakness you can adjust accordingly); it is usual to start on a low number of repetitions and work up.

5 By adjusting the circuit at any time if it starts to become monotonous and you want a change. A further bonus is that by keeping the 'exercise content' constant within the circuit, it is possible to develop stamina by decreasing exercise time gradually.

Sample Circuits
(*starting repetitions in italics*)

Always begin with a preliminary warm-up: jog/run on spot for one minute; rest one minute; jog/run one minute.

Circuit A

Neck rolls (*Sup. 4*) (*10*)
Step-ups (*Str. 15*) (*6*)
Arm flings (*Sup. 8*) (*10*)
Calf raises (*Str. 18*) (*6*)
Bent-leg sit-ups (*Str. 9*) (*4*)
Squat thrusts (*Str. 11*) (*6*)
Shoulder shrugs (*Sup. 5*) (*15*)
Trunk twists (*Sup. 2*) (*6 each side*)
Half squats (*Str. 10*) (*6*)

Circuit B

Shoulder shrugs (*Sup. 5*) (*15*)
Bent-leg sit-ups (*Str. 9*) (*4*)
Knee pulls (*Sup. 14*) (*4 each side*)
Squat thrusts (*Str. 11*) (*6*)
Hip raises (*Str. 3*) (*8*)
Leg swings (*Sup. 13*) (*6 each leg*)
Push-ups, (modified if necessary) (*Str. 1*) (*6*)
Alternate toe-touches (*Sup. 3*) (*6 each side*)
The lunge (*Sup. 11*) (*4 each side*)

Circuit C

Side bends (*Sup. 1*) (*6 each side*)
Push-ups, (modified if necessary) (*Str. 1*) (*6*)
Leg swings (*Sup. 13*) (*6 each leg*)
Squat thrusts (*Str. 11*) (*6*)
Arm flings (*Sup. 8*) (*10*)
Bent-leg sit-ups (*Str. 9*) (*4*)
Shoulder shrugs (*Sup. 5*) (*15*)
Step-ups (*Str. 15*) (*6*)
The lunge (*Sup. 11*) (*4 each side*)

These circuits can be done at home, in the open or in a gymnasium and, if there are facilities available, make use of them (consult the resident instructor on how to incorporate them into your training circuit). But with a bit of ingenuity certain other exercises can also be done at home using everyday or easily obtainable items.

Warming-up and Warming-down

Warming-up

The purpose of warming-up, which is perhaps the single most important element in sports fitness, is twofold:

1 To tune the participant both mentally and physically.
2 To lessen the chance of injuring unprepared muscles.

With time at a premium and sports facilities expensive and in high demand, the tendency for most players is to rush into their sport at maximum power and speed. Nothing could be more calculated to lead to injury. It is essential to warm up beforehand, both physically and mentally and this pays dividends far in excess of the time expended on it. A number of players, especially if accustomed to a warmer climate, take a hot shower before play (a hot bath is too enervating) and raise the body temperature to the most favourable point for intense muscular activity. Warming the muscles relaxes them and improves muscle response; it also has the effect of stretching the muscles and making them less prone to injury if violently used. Mental warm-up is important to ease stress and tension before a match or game and generally to key the mind to the forthcoming test.

Warming-up, for the most part, consists of some jogging (running/jogging on the spot when the former is impracticable) and some simple stretching exercises — particularly of those parts of the body which are most used. Warming-up should be taken to the point of sweating, except in those sports where a lot of waiting is involved.

Method

Carry out six to ten repetitions of general stretching exercises as described on pages 11 to 16. Particularly valuable are:

Arm flings (*Sup. 8*)
Toe touches (*Sup. 3*)
Side bends (*Sup. 1*)
Trunk twists (*Sup. 2*)
The lunge (*Sup. 11*)
Arm circling (*Sup. 7*)
Calf stretch (*Sup. 15*)
Knee pulls (*Sup. 14*)
Wrist shakes (*Sup. 9*)
Neck rolls (*Sup. 4*)

Further details of warming-up exercises are given in Section II.

Warming-down

Warming-down is almost as important in the prevention of incapacitation as warming-up. Cold, damp clothes next to the skin are a prime source of chills and, for the more elderly, could lead to

muscular aches. Particularly susceptible are those parts of the body where clothing has been restricted — the waist, crotch, feet, armpits and back. It is sensible after play to put on a sweater to keep the muscles warm, and to walk about after exercise carrying out a few suppleness exercises to prevent the muscles stiffening up.

The purpose of the warming-down process is to allow the body to cool down gradually. It is also sensible and hygienic to take a shower or bath as soon as you can, and to take the opportunity to massage stiff or sore muscles while they are under water. This applies particularly to the neck and shoulders. If a hot bath or shower is impracticable, a brisk rub with a towel will also help prevent irritating after-sport stiffness.

Weight and Fitness

The weight factor is as significant an element in fitness for sport as it is in general fitness. In sport, if you are overweight you are likely to be short of stamina and will tire sooner than your opponent, but in addition you will also be placing yourself at greater risk through injury. It has been shown conclusively that the more tired a sportsman or sportswoman becomes, the more prone he or she is to injury. For when fatigue strikes concentration lapses, the natural reflexes are blunted, and muscles seem no longer to be mastered by the brain.

In additon, if overweight, you expose yourself to such problems as shortness of breath, varicose veins, backache, arthritis, chest troubles, high blood pressure and diabetes (both these last two can lead to heart conditions), and other ailments and disabilities.

The table below shows a suggested weight to height ratio.

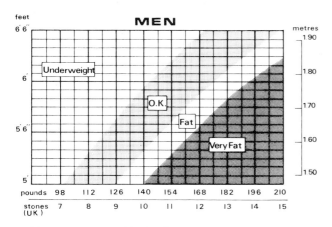

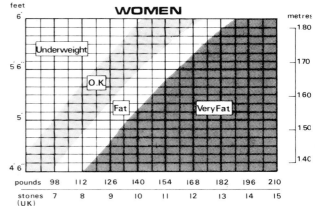

Diagram courtesy Health Education Council

SECTION 2
Fit for Riding

Introduction

Riding is a unique sport, for successful riding depends on a partnership, a harmony between two totally different beings – the rider and his horse.

Fitness for riding calls for the fitness of both elements; however fit the rider, an unfit horse will never be able to perform to his optimum capacity; conversely, an unfit rider will not be able to get the best from his horse and may even cause unnecessary injury to his mount.

The Rider

General Fitness Requirements

As a recreation, riding does not call for the highest level of physical fitness, and riding can be done at all ages and at all levels. But, as the rider becomes more proficient, a parallel increase in fitness is called for, essentially to be fit enough to maintain the correct riding position and to be sufficiently relaxed and balanced on the horse at all times. It is then that the rider can perform with confidence, feeling as one with his horse.

It is the *confident* rider who will inspire confidence in his horse; hence the nervous or tense rider will quickly communicate these feelings to his mount. Further, if a rider is tense he will almost certainly be making life uncomfortable for his horse – often by gripping excessively with his legs or being rough with his hands, or stiff in his back. The all-important *balance* a rider needs is a product of technical proficiency – which comes through perfecting the riding position and is fundamental to being a good rider – and physical fitness.

The Riding Position

The classical riding seat has evolved over many centuries, and is the most economical and practicable method of getting the best out of one's horse. With a correct seat, not only can a rider relax and ride in a balanced posture, but can assist his horse positively.

For riding and schooling on the flat, the essence of the classical seat is that the rider should sit squarely in the lowest part of the saddle with his point of balance immediately above that of the horse – just behind the withers. Taken from the side, it should be possible to draw a line through the rider's ear, shoulder, hip and heel. The shoulder should be relaxed and the rider's weight should be evenly balanced with the feet resting in

The correct riding position
(*photograph* © *Hugo M. Czerny*)

the stirrups. The weight is taken in three places; on the *seat* bones, the *thighs* and the *feet* in the stirrups.

As the stirrups are taken up for jumping or cross-country work, the centre of balance of the rider is altered with more weight being taken on the thighs and stirrups and less on the seat. At the same time the angles – which we will call the riding angles (ankle, knee and hip) are narrowed, while the point of balance is over the stirrups.

The extreme is reached with the flat-race jockey who rides very short with the riding angles closed up. Having his seat, thighs and knees clear of the saddle, he is not able to grip the horse and only the lower part of the leg is in contact, the stirrups taking all his weight.

Rounded back (*left*); hollow back (*centre*); the correct position (*right*)

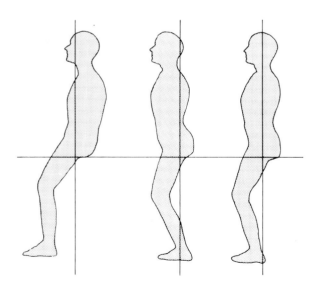

Aids

When the rider has adopted the correct riding position, is sitting balanced, deep in his saddle and relaxed, he can call on certain signals to control the horse. These are known as 'Aids' and are the language of horsemanship. They can be divided into:

natural aids: voice, legs, seat and hands
artificial aids: whips, spurs and any other form of strap, apart from the reins, to control the horse (e.g. the martingale).

For the purposes of rider fitness, however, we need only consider the natural aids: legs, seat and hands. (If the rider cannot use his voice then he has a real fitness problem!)

Legs

The horse is a creature of flight and his instincts are to pull away from contact. It is this characteristic which is the basis of the use of the leg aid. The rider's legs are used to urge the horse to go forward (both legs) or to turn (one leg only). With constant training and work the slightest pressure of the legs will have the desired effect, but the aid must be given strongly enough for the horse to respond.

Seat

The horse is propelled by motive force from the hind legs. This natural movement – known as *impulsion,* (which is defined as 'a tendency to move forward with elasticity, originating from the haunches, flowing into a swinging back and ending in the mouth,') — can be stifled if the rider sits too stiffly or heavily in the saddle. Operating the seat aids — which are almost imperceptible to anyone watching — involves the lower part of the body absorbing the horse's movements but not opposing them.

Hands

Through the reins and the bit, the hands are in direct communication with the horse's head. They must maintain an even, consistent touch, sympathetic but controlled. They must also remain still in relation to the horse's head, irrespective of the movements of the rest of the rider's body.

It is clear that the use of these aids must be highly disciplined. The rider needs to be in control of himself so that when he gives an aid it is a single specific command, a definite signal, not a continuous collection of perhaps involuntary nudges. If for instance the legs are used persistently to urge the horse forward the signal is either responded to in excess or else so confuses the horse that it is eventually ignored. It is essential for a rider when giving aids to discontinue the moment the horse responds. Giving the aid tells the horse what to do, relaxing it tells him that he is doing it correctly and is his reward.

The rider needs to be fit enough and supple enough to absorb the movement and swing of the horse's back with his own body and be able to sit relaxed and deep in the saddle; yet still able to give distinct signals to the horse through the legs, seat and hands acting independently of each other.

Paces

So far we have discussed the general principles of riding. There are, however, specific requirements for the different paces of the horse.

Walk

This is a four-time pace. Although each leg moves independently of the others in four equal beats and in set sequence, the horse's back moves forward in a series of intervals of equal length but not at constant speed. This variation of speed must be absorbed by the lower part of the back of the rider.

At walk the horse's head will nod as each foreleg hits the ground and the rider must be at pains not to interfere with this movement through the reins. In fact, the hands must act independently of the rider's body, able to follow the movements of the horse's head yet maintaining control and feel by even contact. In addition, as the horse walks, his rib cage sways slightly from side to side and the rider must absorb this movement too. Not by swinging from side to side in unison as many novices do, but by sitting softly and deeply in the saddle.

Trot

This is a two-time pace with each diagonal pair of the horse's legs striking the ground alternately and there is a time when all four feet are off the ground together; this is known as the moment of suspension. The beginner will inevitably bounce in the saddle in response to this unusual movement of the horse and one of the first lessons for a novice is to rise correctly to the trot.

In this the rider takes himself off the saddle when one diagonal pair of legs is in contact with the ground, and returns to the saddle when it is the turn of the other pair.

Later comes the *sitting trot*. In this, the rider has to absorb the horse's movements in his hips and back, while his shoulders and elbows must be relaxed so that his hands remain still.

Canter

This is a three-time pace with the horse's legs working in the following sequence: one hind leg, the other and its diagonal pair, and then the last foreleg. This results in a pronounced rocking effect like that of a rocking chair; in addition, there is a moment of suspension. In canter, there is considerably more movement of the horse's back than in either walk or trot, and this extra movement must be absorbed through the rider's hips, and not by swinging the upper part of the body backwards and forwards, as is so often the case.

Gallop

Gallop is a faster version of canter and is a four-time pace (with the diagonal sequence of canter broken). In many respects this is the easiest pace to ride correctly as the rider's seat is usually out of the saddle and he is balanced over the stirrups.

Jumping

In jumping, as with gallop, more weight is taken on the stirrups, and the stirrup leathers are shortened accordingly to reduce the riding

angles. Over the fence the rider is still balanced over the stirrups having his back straight rather than rounded, bending from the hip.

At the apex of the fence the horse does an accentuated rocking movement and the riding angles close up even more. On landing the rider returns gently to the saddle as the riding angles increase again.

Levels of Riding Fitness

Riders who wish to ride only occasionally or are forced to become week-end riders do not need a high level of fitness, but should be fit enough so as not to be unduly stiff and sore afterwards. To prevent stiffness a few suppleness exercises, particularly for the back and leg muscles – calves and thighs – would be beneficial (*see p. 16*). The most important thing to prevent soreness and rubbing is to have correctly fitting breeches and boots (*see below*).

Another possible characteristic of the occasional rider is to be overweight. An overweight rider is very apt to be short of breath and to tire easily, and having a tired rider is a pronounced handicap for the horse. In addition, an overweight rider will probably be top heavy, and this will make the horse's task that much more difficult when trying to recover from a bad mistake or stumble.

A further disadvantage too is that a horseman's choice of mount will be severely limited. A lighter rider might choose a thoroughbred, a twenty-stone man will have to go for something like a cart-horse!

Position of the body when jumping
(photograph © Findlay Davidson)

Endurance Riding, Trekking, Long-distance Riding and Hunting

If the rider has not been in the saddle for some time, the many saddle hours involved in any form of cross-country riding will be felt in almost every part of the body — especially in the small of the back, hamstrings and calves. If not truly fit, a day's hunting will prove decidedly uncomfortable, and if it is uncomfortable for the rider it will almost certainly be uncomfortable for the horse.

When a tired rider bounces about in the saddle and loses his riding position it upsets the horse's rhythm and further, sets up movement in opposition to the horse's own movements. Thus the rider will have to grip with his legs to stay balanced.

If physically tired, one is less able to help one's horse, concentration slackens, suppleness begins to go, everything in effect becomes more brittle. In addition, reactions become slower, body and limbs are less responsive and joints can stiffen up. Once muscular elasticity is lost, the rider becomes less relaxed and the essential harmony with the horse disappears altogether.

The tired rider is likely to be off balance before his horse makes a mistake (like hitting a fence or pecking on landing) and will be even more off balance when it occurs. If this is the case, the horse is quite likely to fall, whereas a fit rider sitting properly would be in a position to aid his horse's recovery.

Every horse is different. One horse might be very easy and pleasant to ride at sitting trot but uncomfortable at canter. Another might be the reverse. Yet another might take a tremendous hold when he gallops and half pull one's arms from their sockets. One's degree of fitness must accord with the horse one rides.

Dressage and Schooling

Dressage is a very controlled form of riding. It is fundamental in horse training and calls for a strong sense of discipline for both horse and rider. To the uninitiated, dressage appears almost a separate riding art, but, in fact, the principles of dressage apply to all forms of riding and are basic to an understanding of the horse in action.

The object of dressage is to develop the horse's natural movements in a controlled and calm way so as to promote rhythm and balance. In effect, it is a form of gymnastic training for the horse which is designed to develop the muscles of his body and lead to all-round fitness and a better partnership with his rider. It also makes the rider supremely conscious of, and sensitive to, the requirements of his horse.

Dressage calls essentially for suppleness on the part of the rider so he can be as relaxed as possible. Although a dressage training session may last only 30 minutes or so – to avoid a horse becoming tired or for that matter bored with constant repetition work (*see below*) – they are minutes of intense concentration. To remain relaxed under such pressure calls for a fairly high level of general fitness.

The Fitness Needs of Riding

To summarise, the rider therefore needs a reasonable level of –
1   *General fitness* – including not being overweight.
2   *Stamina* – heart and lung endurance.
3   *Strength* – enough strength to maintain the correct riding position and to control the horse using appropriate aids, with the maximum amount of self-control and the minimum amount of force.
4   *All-round body suppleness*.

Stamina-building Exercises

See p. 24 for general stamina-building exercises and session durations, etc.

Much favoured by riders are –

Running
Swimming
Skiing   (excellent too for strengthening and using the riding muscles.)
Bicycling   (A popular form of bicycling is to bicycle standing up. This is an extremely exhausting exercise and it is as well to ease yourself into it. Start with 200-300 metres alternately sitting and standing. Lengthen the distances progressively.)

Strength Exercises

See p. 17 for general strength exercises. But these should aim particularly at the:

Shoulders
Back (especially the lower back)
Riding muscles (inside the upper leg)
Calves

Suppleness Exercises

See p. 11 for general suppleness exercises. Suppleness is really needed all over the body, especially in:

Wrists
Hands
Hips
Knees
Ankles
Back

Exercise Circuits

Details of the conduct of an exercise circuit will be found on p. 25. Below are a number of possible circuits: numbers in italics are *starting* repetitions.

Circuit A

Preliminary warm-up: jogging/running on the spot – one minute; rest – one minute; run on the spot – one minute.

Shoulder shrugs (Sup. 5) (*15*)
Leg swings (Sup. 13) (*6 each side*)
Neck rolls (Sup. 4) (*10*)
Half squats (Str. 10) (*6*)
Wrist shakes (Sup. 9) (*15 seconds*)
Arm circles (Sup. 7) (*6*)
Bench jumps (Str. 16) (*6*)
Bent-leg sit-ups (Str. 9) (*4*)

Circuit B

Preliminary warm-up: jogging/running on the spot – one minute; rest – one minute; run on the spot – one minute.

Arm flings (Sup. 8) (*10*)
Neck rolls (Sup. 4) (*10*)
Bent-leg sit-ups (Str. 9) (*4*)
Wrist shakes (Sup. 9) (*15 seconds*)
'Bicycling' (Str. 8) (10 seconds)
Shoulder shrugs (Sup. 5) (*15*)
Side bends (Sup. 1) (*6 each side*)
Leg swings (Sup. 13) (*6 each side*)
Trunk twists (Sup. 2) (*6 each side*)

Casual Limbering-up

In addition, it is well worth doing some casual limbering up before riding or waiting for an event to start. This can be done either on the ground or on horseback.
Useful exercises include :

Neck rolls (Sup. 4)
Arm flings (Sup. 8)
Wrist shakes (Sup. 9)
Leg swings (Sup. 13)
Trunk twists (Sup. 2)

Mental Attitude

The horse has very acute senses and an extremely retentive memory. This combination makes it possible in the first place to train him but, as an inevitable product of his training, he learns to rely on and to trust his rider. In consequence, the rider must be consistent, must never betray his horse's trust and must realise as well as understand the responsibility he has towards his horse.

Riding is a team effort between horse and rider and at top levels of competition this becomes of paramount importance. Mind over matter may work for human beings, but it does not work to the same extent with the horse. The rider must be in tune with his horse. He must be level-headed and not get over-excited. He must inspire confidence in the horse to get him to do what he wants, and he cannot impose his will on his horse as he might on his own body. A human being will put up with discomfort and pain both in training and competition to achieve a particular objective, whereas a horse cannot rationalise in this way. He will make a comparable effort only if he enjoys what he is doing or is faced with a competitive situation which he understands. It is, therefore, harmony between horse and rider and the confidence that this brings to the horse that can produce the right effect. Coercion is usually counter-productive.

At top level, many riders crack under the strain or show signs of stress before competition. If a rider is tense or nervous it is very quickly communicated to the horse. It is not clear whether this is felt physically, through some sixth sense or by some other telepathic means – but it happens just the same. It also follows that if a rider is calm and relaxed this is passed on to his mount. Furthermore, time and time again it has been shown that the rider who can remain in control of his own emotions, and who can communicate confidently and consistently with his horse using the same aids he normally employs in training, will produce the best results in competition.

Avoiding Injury

There is little doubt that the less fit the rider the more prone he is to injury. When tired, in particular, a rider will start to lose his riding position and will try to maintain himself in the saddle through gripping rather than by balance. Once this occurs, he will keep muscles under constant tension and there is no surer way to muscle injury. On the other hand, if a horse makes a bad mistake the fit rider will try to stay in balance with his mount for as long as possible to give him every chance to recover.

(© *Gerald Broadhead*)

Falling

If a horse falls, however, there does come a moment for the rider to part company and roll clear. There are obviously occasions when the rider should bale out quite early in the fall, particularly if he is likely to be trapped under his

42

horse. When falling, the rider should be as relaxed as possible on hitting the ground – easier said than done and very difficult to practise! But he must be prepared to roll or leap clear if necessary.

A horse will do his best to avoid treading on a rider but, if he is struggling to get up, his hooves can fly in all directions. (A few lessons in judo are invaluable in learning to fall without injury.)

Clothing

Hats

A correctly fitting, hard riding hat is essential – correctly fitting means that it will not fall off when the rider falls! There is a tendency to use a chinstrap with a peaked cap. If the peak is fixed this could, in certain circumstances, lead to a broken neck i.e. if the hat is jerked upwards in a fall. It is therefore advisable to have a flexible peak if a chinstrap is worn.

Boots

Riding boots are made of leather, rubber or PVC.

Leather boots: These are substantially more expensive than the other types and require upkeep to maintain their suppleness. When well kept, however, they provide the best support and as they mould to the shape of the foot and calf are far and away the most comfortable.

It is essential to keep leather boots clean, for horse sweat contains a high level of salts and on drying will cause them to become brittle. This calls for occasional oiling to keep the boots supple, but not so much oiling that they lose their body and become too soft.

Rubber boots: these are quite popular, are, of course, waterproof and require no upkeep. But they are inclined to be hot in summer and cold in winter and they lack the substance and support of leather.

PVC boots: these are also waterproof and they look like leather. Further, they require no upkeep. However, they become very slippery when wet and will never mould to the shape of the foot as will leather.

Whatever the composition of the boot, a number of factors are of great importance in the interest of safety:—
1   The boot must have a heel, to prevent the foot from slipping through the stirrup.
2   If a leather boot requires resoling, ensure that a complete sole is fitted. Otherwise there will be a ridge and, if the half-sole comes away, the stirrup could be caught in the boot.
3   The soles should not be nailed, nor should they be ridged – which is why it is so dangerous to ride in most forms of gum boot.

Breeches

Old-fashioned woollen breeches required scrubbing by hand in cool water and this has made them unpopular. They have been largely superceded by synthetic or nylon breeches which will not shrink noticeably. However, they must be comfortable and not too loose, nor too large for they will then wrinkle where the legs come in contact with the saddle and cause rubbing.

Breeches should be large enough to enable the rider to wear something underneath them in cold weather. Sometimes it is necessary to wear nylon tights, to prevent rubbing, whatever the weather conditions.

Hunting Tie (Stock)

It is sensible to wear a hunting tie or stock when riding cross-country. Apart from being an article of fashion it provides warmth and protection for the neck.

Gloves

Grip and warmth are the two criteria in choice of gloves. Hogskin are best for work on the flat, when riding a horse which does not sweat much, or in summer. In winter and in wet weather, string or woollen gloves are preferable.

Back Protectors

Back protectors are very important to reduce the chance of injury to the back in cross-country riding. They are comfortable and light and can prevent a serious back injury.

Tack

All tack must be properly maintained, not just for the sake of cleanliness, but also for safety reasons. Tack should be inspected regularly and any stitching showing signs of wear *must* be repaired immediately.

The Saddle

It is essential that the saddle fits both rider and horse.

For the rider it must basically fit well enough so that in the correct riding position it will be comfortable – if it isn't, the rider will soon enough know as it will rub and cause discomfort. This means that a saddle must be broad enough across the seat, must not be too wide nor too narrow in the arch, nor too big or short from pommel to cantel. In addition, it must accommodate the rider's thighs and knees.

For the horse, within the limits above, the bearing surface on the horse's back must be as big as possible. It must not tip from front to back nor roll from side to side. In general, the saddle must fit closely to the horse without pressing on his spine or his withers. An ill-fitting or badly padded saddle will very quickly make the horse's back sore. So it is important to regularly check the padding to ensure that it is not becoming lumpy or too compressed.

Leathers

For safety, these should be unbreakable, and raw hide ones are the most popular. These, however, do have a tendency to stretch, usually unequally and, if this is not corrected, could have an effect on the riding position. Stainless steel buckles, although expensive, are the safest.

Stirrups

The stirrups must be of the correct size for the boot. Not too big, otherwise there is a danger of the foot slipping through, not too small in case the foot gets jammed. If the bearing surface is worn down, the boot is likely to slip. In this event, rubber stirrup treads can be fitted – these are also warmer and more comfortable. Stainless steel stirrups are the most reliable.

Bitting

Bitting is a complex and neglected subject, yet it is of crucial importance for both the control and the comfort of a horse. In some cases it will require an expert to find the right bit for a horse but, in principle, the horse must be comfortable in his mouth, not frightened of the bit and willing to accept its contact.

One should always use the mildest bit with which one can comfortably control the horse, bearing in mind that, if the bit is too mild, the horse will be too strong for the rider and the hand aids will have to be correspondingly rougher. It is often more comfortable for the horse to have a stronger bit so that the rider can ride more easily and quietly.

The bit should be neither too wide nor too narrow for the jaw – if the former, there will be too much leverage and pressure on the jaw; if the latter, the horse's mouth may be pinched. In general, the thicker the bit the milder.

If the bit is too strong, the horse may resent it. This will cause him to throw his head around, trying to evade it. Such actions will cause other resistances through his body and these are incompatible with the ultimate fitness and well-being of the horse.

The Horse

General

In the wild, roaming as do other herbivores in search of food, water and safety, the horse keeps himself very fit in the battle for survival. He is an animal who ranges over a large area, an animal of flight using wide open spaces and he has a well-developed herd instinct. Yet, in most civilised countries, he is cooped up in a comparatively small paddock which restricts his activities. It is little wonder that many horses, overfed in lush paddocks with no necessity to search for food become fat, soft and out of condition – only too often like their owners!

The horse is essentially a very athletic, versatile creature, but it is asking a lot of him to perform many different functions under controlled conditions and to do them to the utmost of his ability – all with a weight on his back. Horses, like any athlete, are prone to injury – and their forelegs are particularly vulnerable – but they are far more prone when unfit or tired.

A horse coming back into work off grass is often overweight and too much of that weight is fat and not muscle. If the ground in his paddock is soft, not only his muscles, but also his tendons and ligaments, will be soft and out of trim. As an unfit horse is also prone to injury, it is important that any fitness programme be taken easily and gradually from the start.

A schedule to bring a horse to peak fitness can take up to 3½ months.

(© *Gerald Broadhead*)

Bringing a Horse to Peak Fitness

This is basically a guide to training, and the programme can be modified depending on the facilities available and the terrain — for instance the more hilly the country the harder the horse will work in a given time. Throughout this training it must be a primary aim to build and develop a rapport between horse and rider.

The 3½ month period is divided into:—
Preliminary work: weeks 1 to 4
Development work: weeks 5 to 9
Fast work: weeks 10 to 14

Preliminary Work (Four Weeks)

Preliminary work is designed gradually to exercise the horse and begin the process of turning fat into muscle while burning up any extra fat he has gained when out of work, and it is a slow process. It is also to tone up the muscles, tendons and ligaments, and to harden the legs. Road work at walk will achieve this. Initially, it is best to start on flat ground, progressing to work uphill and, after two weeks, including some gentle trotting uphill. This exercises the muscles more, whereas trotting on the flat can cause unnecessary jarring to the horse's legs which, in an unfit horse, could lead to leg problems.

Duration: a gradual start (30 minutes daily) is best, building up 10-15 minutes until the optimum of 1½-2 hours' roadwork is reached. (If the terrain is hilly the same amount of work can be achieved in a shorter time.)

If short-cuts are taken at this early stage, the horse is much more susceptible to injury. In particular, if the rider starts galloping straight away he could strain the animal's heart, cause wind troubles and, above all, damage the horse's legs which at this stage are very vulnerable to tendon and ligament strain.

Development Work (Fifth Week onwards)

By the end of the fourth week of roadwork with some uphill trotting towards the end of the period, the horse should be ready to go to the next stage of his training. It is now time to incorporate suppling exercises and cantering, yet still maintaining a certain amount of roadwork as well.

Development training varies of course. For the polo pony this will include basic schooling, with some stick and ball exercises; the show jumper will be jumping small fences and combinations of fences; the race horse will be cantering; the long-distance horse will be stepping up its work programme; while the event horse will be concentrating on suppling exercises — circles, turns and a variety of basic gymnastic exercises on the flat as part of his dressage training and in preparation for his jumping, which can be started about a fortnight later.

Seventh week onwards: the time has come to start building up the horse's stamina — heart and lung endurance — by cantering on the flat and, better still, uphill (the value of uphill work is that the horse thrusts more with his hind legs placing less pressure on his forelegs).

Jumping starts with gymnastic work over small fences to get the jumping muscles in trim. This may be done two to three times a week and gradually more can be asked of the horse in each session, while the jumps can become larger as the horse becomes fitter.

There is a tendency for an inexperienced rider to jump fences that suit himself rather than jumping those that suit the needs of the horse. This is wrong. The individual needs of the horse are paramount. If a rider wants to improve his technique, practise jumping for his own satisfaction, jump to recover his nerve or just jump for the hell of it, and if this is going to be at the expense of the horse, he *must* find another mount.

Fast Work (Ninth to Tenth Week onwards)

The training regime has now been in operation for eight to nine weeks and the time has come to progress to the next stage of the horse's training, namely to build up to peak fitness. By now he should be reasonably hard, reasonably supple, and much of his excess fat should have been converted to muscle, although there may still be some flesh to lose. Hopefully, he is bubbling with enthusiasm and keen on his work.

This enthusiasm is closely linked with the horse's understanding of what he is doing and with what he is wanting to do. Hunting, polo, racing and similar activities are fun for the horse. He enjoys the sport, enjoys galloping with other horses, for it appeals to his herd instinct. He finds such work exhilirating and he feels he is getting somewhere. On the other hand, too much repetition work and continuous work on a circular track may make him lose interest but, should a horse be very excitable, such repetition work could be just the thing to settle him. Every horse is different and the art of training a horse is to understand his mentality, treat him as an individual and tailor his training programme accordingly.

Galloping: this is particularly relevant to the racehorse and the event horse – in other equestrian sports the horse may be brought to the peak level of fitness required by actual participation, albeit without over-exertion at first. However, galloping will reveal the true state of the horse's fitness, and his rate of recovery can be monitored.

Recovery rate will be slower in hot or humid weather than it will be in frosty or cool conditions. At the same time, it is important to listen to see how clean he is in his wind and examine if the discharge from his nose is clear or thick.

Over the next three weeks the horse should work on the gallops between one and three times a week, and after this the horse should be nearing his peak fitness. But there should always be something in reserve. In training, a horse should never be at full stretch and, at all costs, over-exertion should be avoided. It is far better to have a horse 95 per cent fit and 100 per cent well, than the reverse.

After-exercise Care

After exercise, the horse should be allowed to unwind *slowly*. Quiet walking after fast work, for 20-30 minutes, gives the horse's pulse rate a chance to slow down gradually, his wind to recover, his muscles to relax and his metabolism to return to normal.

Body temperature control is an important element in the unwinding process after finishing work, above all the horse must not be allowed to become chilled. Nor, for that matter in very hot weather must he remain hot for too long. In extreme cases of overheating a horse's temperature must be brought down as quickly as possible – by hosing or applying ice packs.

In normal conditions, however, he should be rubbed down as soon after work as possible – if during cold weather rubbing down is delayed he should be rugged up, and if he has been sweating a lot, a sweat rug should be put on first. The sweat should be removed by sponging or scraping – particularly from under the saddle, and in the areas of the girths and bridle – and the horse should be dried thoroughly.

He will want to drink after exercise and he should be allowed to do so, but only half a bucket at a time until his thirst is satisfied. Many horses benefit from being turned out in a field and this is excellent for the unwinding process as well as for general mental relaxation. But he must have first quenched his thirst and not be turned out immediately after exercise. Very lush and wet grass should be avoided as this could lead to colic (*see below*). However, by turning a horse out to grass, many digestive disorders can be avoided and the horse is able to balance his food naturally with the requisite amount of exercise he has taken. Perhaps the best is to work the horse in the morning, give him his water and hay after exercise and then at a later stage turn him out in the field.

Clipping

It may not be necessary to clip a horse in winter time for the first few weeks of work unless he is sweating a lot. When exercise becomes more intense, or the horse starts to sweat under his winter coat, he should be clipped, otherwise he is prone to becoming chilled. Many people prefer to start with a trace or blanket clip according to need, but with a full clip it is normal to leave a saddle patch to prevent rubbing. If the horse lives outdoors his legs should be unclipped and he should be appropriately rugged.

Grooming

A well-kept horse is well groomed. In the worst event a dirty saddle on a sweaty horse will scald his back and rub at the girth, and this could lead to blisters, even girth galls, which will prevent any riding until cured. Brushing off dried sweat, particularly if it has been on the horse for several hours, can be very irritating to him but if it is first washed out of his coat and then he is dried thoroughly, he will be more comfortable and, further, he is less likely to break out in sweat later.

Grooming is an important part of the fitness process as it acts as a massage to tone up the skin and muscles near the surface, as well as ensuring that the coat and skin are clean.

Keeping Your Horse Fit and Healthy

Observation is the key to keeping your horse healthy. Every horse is an individual and only someone who knows him well can recognise if his behaviour is unusual. Only by knowing the normal horse will one be able to spot early warning signs of disease. Whenever possible, quietly observe him in stable or paddock. First of all check him without being seen, taking in his general posture and attitude. As one approaches one should note his reactions, facial expressions, alertness or otherwise. Once one is happy about

(© *Gerald Broadhead*)

his general attitude, he should be led around and checked for lameness, and injuries. A horse should be observed closely at least once a day when living out and more often when stabled. It is during these inspections that one is most likely to recognise something amiss. The following points should be checked.

Head

The eye should be open, bright, clear and with no discharge. Any other changes, such as blueing of the cornea, should be noted. The condition of the mucous membranes (the linings of the eyes, the mouth, and with a mare, the vulva) is a useful guide to the well-being of a horse. The membranes should be moist. The linings of the eye, for example, should be salmon-pink; if pale, this can indicate anaemia; if blueish, the circulation may be poor; if dark red, it usually denotes illness.

Breathing

To determine the rate, the nostrils and the flanks should be watched. The nostrils flare and contract with each breath and the flank can just be seen rising and falling. The normal horse breathes smoothly, regularly, and effortlessly 8 to 20 times per minute. Only in hot, humid weather will horses breathe fast, when they may reach rates of up to 40 times per minute. Distress, both physical or otherwise, can increase the respiratory rate.

Smell the breath — it should be sweet. A foetid smell may denote a tooth or sinus problem. The mucous membranes (the lining of the nostrils must be checked). They should be moist and free from discharge. The nostrils should not be flared.

Skin

The skin should be elastic. One should be able to pull out a pinch of skin on the horse's neck and when released, it should quickly return to its original position. If the horse is dehydrated, the skin will return slowly and will tend to stay in folds.

The coat should be shiny and not dull. The skin should be free of lesions or parasites, e.g. lice, ringworm, bot eggs, and warbles.

Body Heat

If one places the flat of one's hand on the horse, one can soon learn to judge a horse's temperature, but to become proficient it must be done every day. After a time one will be able to spot a fever without a thermometer.

If this is suspected his temperature should be taken. The normal body temperature of the horse is around 100.5°F (38°C), although this can vary one degree either way. Temperature can also vary with the time of day, exercise, hot weather, pain or illness. The temperature should be taken when the horse has been at rest for some time in order to give an accurate reading.

Taking a Horse's Pulse

When determining a horse's pulse rate one should wait until he is relaxed and rested, then place one's fingers on the artery under the jaw for 30 seconds and multiply the beat by two. The heart rate or pulse varies with the age of the horse, but adult horses generally have a pulse rate of 28 to 40 beats per minute. Disease can cause this to rise to over 100 beats per minute.

Gut Noises

By placing one's ear to the horse's flank, one can hear gut sounds – the noises of the normal contractions and relaxations of the gut. Absence or excess of these sounds can indicate a problem.

Dung

Most horses defaecate every two hours or so, although this is more frequent when the animal is excited. The droppings should be light brown to dark-green in colour, depending on diet, and should break when they hit the ground. Loose droppings can be caused by excitement, variation in diet – particularly if this is too rich – or through disease e.g. bacterial or parasite infections. If there is a marked change in consistency or smell it should be noted.

Urine

A horse's urine should be yellowy-brown, but may vary in colour and thickness. Bloody or coffee-coloured urine should be drawn immediately to the attention of a vet.

Injuries

When walking around one's horse one should look for swellings and injuries. By running one's hands all over the body, but especially between the ears and down and in between the legs, it is often possible to detect something abnormal.

Lameness

Many injuries and lamenesses start in a small way and if recognised early can be prevented from becoming more serious. A mere bruise if undetected may, with work, soon develop into a strain which could require months of treatment.

It is particularly important to check a horse's legs regularly – early in the morning, before and after exercise and at evening stables. The legs should be firm and not puffy. Particular note should be taken of any heat, or swelling.

In cases of severe lameness, the affected leg is obvious. The horse will favour it, and place his weight on the opposite sound leg. In less severe cases, however, it is sometimes difficult to tell which is the affected leg. Under these circumstances, the horse should be taken onto hard level ground and led at a trot straight away from an observer and then straight back again. Any deviation in pace can then usually be seen. It is important to realise that a lame animal takes as much weight as possible off the injured leg and places extra weight on the sound one and, as a result, the head rises as the affected leg hits the ground, whereas it sinks on the sound one. In addition, he will usually step shorter on the affected leg.

The pulse strength often gives a clue as to the injured leg, as indeed can the presence of heat. It is also worth remembering that there is always a mirror image on the other side of the horse, for comparison with the suspect leg. Feeling the leg carefully will also help find the painful spot. Always bear in mind that if one works a horse with a developing lameness, a slight problem can very easily turn into something more serious. It is best to err on the cautious side at all times.

Some Important Conditions

Colic

Colic is the collective name for abdominal pains in the horse. The causes of colic are numerous:

parasitic damage, injudicious feeding and watering, bed eating and dental problems, being some of the most common. Nervous excitement can also give rise to colic, especially in the young horse.

Symptoms: heart rate and body temperature often increase. The horse may sweat, often profusely. The horse is restless and walks his box, frequently lying down and getting up again. He often arches his back, rolls, kicks his belly and looks round at his flank. The horse may not defaecate for several hours and the droppings may be different from normal.

Treatment: colic can be fatal and prompt action and veterinary help is essential. It can occur at any time and it is important to have discussed with your vet what first aid measures he advises to manage the colic before he arrives. If the horse is thrashing around and damaging himself, he must be restrained on a bridle or head collar, but do not exhaust him by excessive walking.

Prevention: colic cases can be minimised by proper management, especially feeding, watering and exercise – and, of course, parasitic control.

Azoturia (Monday Morning Disease)

Azoturia often occurs when a horse works after a period of rest when there has been no corresponding reduction in feed.

Symptoms: muscle stiffness, tremors, pain and sweating. If exercise continues, these symptoms become very severe. In acute cases the horse is unable to move and may even go down. Urine is often reddish-brown, sometimes black.

Treatment: Work must be *stopped immediately* and a vet called. The horse should be boxed home. Sodium bicarbonate in the water is a useful first-aid measure.

Remember: *If it is suspected that a horse is lame or ill and one cannot see any obvious and easily remedied cause, one should call in a veterinary surgeon immediately.*

Preventative Medicine

Tetanus, Influenza and Rhinopneumonitis

Tetanus: any wound, however small, can put a horse at risk from tetanus, and it is often fatal. However, the vaccine is very effective.

Influenza: this causes coughing and can put a horse out of action for some time. Vaccinations are compulsory for some competition horses. Two initial doses of combined tet/flu vaccine are usually given not less than 21 days and not more than 92 days apart and booster vaccinations are carried out at intervals of no more than 12 months.

Rhinopneumonitis: this causes one of the coughs and one type of abortion. It can be prevented by vaccination.

Worming

Worms cause extensive damage and loss of condition. Horses should be treated every six weeks, alternating between different wormers to minimise resistance. Before treating, it is worth seeking veterinary advice concerning the appropriate medication. Paddock management is also important in this connection (*see below*).

External Parasites

Ticks, mites, biting flies and lice, can be kept under control using washes and other medicines dispensed by a vet.

Dental Care

Proper dental care is an important and often neglected aspect of horse management. If the horse is uncomfortable in his mouth he may not accept the bit and may be unhappy in his work. Bad teeth and dental problems can also result in poor mastication which can lead to colic or to the horse refusing to eat.

The horse may play with his food before eating and swallowing. Feed may fall out of his mouth (quidding). He may appear uncomfortable, one-sided and evade or play with the bit.

A horse's teeth continue to grow throughout his life and need rasping regularly. A vet should check the teeth at least once a year, and preferably twice, especially in young horses.

Wolf Teeth: these are small vestigial teeth located in front of the pre-molars. The bit hitting the wolf teeth can be extemely uncomfortable for the horse, and they are better removed.

Hoof Care

Stabled horses should have their feet checked and picked out at least twice a day. The coronary band should be examined for any injury or pus. Any damage to the hoof wall and sole such as sand cracks should be noted. A foul smelling discharge from the clefts of the frog indicates thrush which often accompanies poor management. The affected area should be cleaned and treated on veterinary advice.

Corns: bruises to the seat of corn (the area under the points of the shoe) which are caused by ill-fitting shoes that have been left on too long. They can be prevented by regular shoeing and trimming. A horse's foot is continually growing, but the shoe cannot change shape. Therefore, unless the shoe is removed and the foot trimmed regularly, it will soon press and bruise the seat of corn causing discoloration. Pockets of blood form and these may go septic, resulting in an abscess at the bulb of the heel. The septic area must be cut out and the wound dressed regularly to draw out all inflammation. In order to keep pressure off the infected area, the hoof should be surgically shod.

Pus in the foot: penetration wounds allow infection to enter the sole, particularly in wet conditions. The foot must be searched and the abcess drained. Poulticing or hot tubbing will help draw out the pus. The tetanus status should always be checked and when the infection is resolved, the foot may need shoeing with a pad.

Feeding

Correct feeding comes only with experience; so if in doubt, one should consult a vet or nutritionist. Details of feeding are really outside the scope of this book, nevertheless several reputable firms produce balanced, cubed rations for horses in work. The primary rule on horse feeding is that the food intake *must balance* the work output.

A horse should finish feeding a good hour before work, and before a rest day it is advisable to cut down his food and introduce bran, to prevent such diseases as azoturia. In addition, hay should not be fed in the two hours before exercise. A horse should be fed from two to four times a day, on a little-and-often basis. Should he bolt his food, place several large, smooth pebbles at the bottom of his manger with his rock salt.

Hay must be well made, and should not be dusty. Dusty hay can affect a horse's wind and the mould spores it contains can cause allergic respiratory problems. Dry matter silage is now marketed in plastic bales and this provides an excellent alternative to hay, particularly if the horse is allergic to dust.

Stables

Stables should be warm and well ventilated. An even temperature is desirable and there should be no draughts. Bedding should be comfortable and adequate. Straw is the traditional material but some horses are allergic to both straw and hay, in which case shavings, peat, or shredded newspaper are useful bedding substitutes. The horse should have continuous access to water, except immediately before exercise.

The aim is to have a happy horse interested in his environment and with enough going on around him so as not to be bored. (Elizabethans, for example, often had a dove-cote in the stable yard). Horses like the companionship of their fellows and often do better if stabled near one another. At morning and evening stables the following points should be checked:

Check for eating up.
Check water consumption and that there is no dung in the water bucket or automatic drinker.
Check hay for dust, weeds, foreign bodies.
Check walls for marks where he may have been cast.
Check the box hasn't been walked or the bed stirred up.

Paddocks

It is important to be aware that horses are notoriously selective grazers. They graze closer than cattle but leave patches where they have defaecated and urinated. The grass grows long and coarse on these patches. To keep paddocks at their best, they should be topped regularly, and if possible grazed with other stock in rotation, e.g. cattle or sheep, which will also provide biological parasite control. Wherever possible, sow an approved seed mixture for horses. This will contain a mixture of grasses, clovers and deep-rooted herbs. Slow release fertilizers (such as those based on fish meal) should be used in preference to artificials.

(© *Gerald Broadhead*)

SECTION 3
Ailments and Injuries

Riding injuries

Introduction

Any physical exertion can cause a variety of aches and pains and this is as true with sport as with any other exercise. Each sport has its own spectrum of typical ailments and injuries, for the most part caused by sudden trauma or repeated wear and tear. Some can be prevented by having a good degree of prior fitness and training, but sportswomen and sportsmen are well advised to know something of the specific injuries that they could sustain when playing their chosen sport.

Specific Injuries Associated with Riding

The illustration indicates the range of injuries which may happen when riding. Some riders may go through their entire riding careers without either experiencing them or coming in contact with them, and bear in mind that fitness renders many muscular injuries far less likely. However, accidents can happen and the medical advice below could be of considerable importance in reducing the effect of injury.

Most serious riding injuries result from falls, with severe head or neck injury being the most dangerous. However, bruising, sprains, strains, dislocations and fractures are all likely consequences, depending on the nature of the fall. There is the added risk of being kicked or trodden upon. In the saddle, the rider can suffer back strain, whiplash neck injury, and sprained ligaments from awkward landings.

Head Injury

A common and potentially very serious hazard for the rider. The risk is of concussion, a temporary loss of function caused by jarring of the brain (*see p. 71*); contusion, or bruising of brain substance (*see p. 71*); or compression, the most dangerous consequence of all — life-threatening increase in brain pressure caused by a haemorrhage inside the skull (*see p. 71*).

Concussion may only cause a few minutes or hours of feeling slightly dazed, but if a rider suffers repeated minor concussions there is a cumulative effect akin to the 'punch-drunk' syndrome of chronic brain-damage that is the legacy of so many boxers. Almost any fall from a horse involves some jarring of the brain, whether the head strikes the ground first or not. Added to that is the risk of having one's head kicked or trodden upon.

An adeqate riding hat is vital but even that is only partially effective in preventing concussion. This is because the head still suffers jarring on direct or indirect trauma.

Treatment: (*See also p. 71*); if conscious, the rider should be kept under supervision for 48 hours after a bad knock on the head, and under close observation if knocked out at all. The level of consciousness, rate of breathing and size of the pupils and their reaction to light, all give an early warning of brain compression.

If unconscious, attention should first be paid to the rider's airway and breathing. If necessary, the jaw should be held forwards to lift the tongue off the back of the throat. Do not move the casualty unless absolutely necessary since there is always the risk of a broken neck and damage to the spinal cord resulting in permanent paralysis.

Life-threatening brain compression can occur *several hours* after a head injury, despite apparent full recovery. Medical attention must be sought urgently at the first signs of *drowsiness* or *confusion, double vision, headache or sickness*.

A frequent characteristic is that the victim of concussion will not admit to feeling peculiar or unwell, indeed will often belligerently protest that he is perfectly all right. It can be up to 48 hours before the full extent of the damage can become apparent, but any sign of strange behaviour or the symptoms of compression listed above must be watched out for. Should they occur the rider must be put to bed, kept quiet and nothing done to alter his level of consciousness — stimulants like coffee or tea, and alcohol can be extremely dangerous.

Note: any loss of consciousness, even for a few seconds, is a danger sign of possible complications.

If knocked out one should not attempt to drive a car for at least a week, and not expose oneself to the risk of a fall for a month or longer.

Neck Injury

A fall, perhaps associated with a head injury but not necessarily so, a kick, or a whiplash injury in the saddle, are the likely causes of pulled muscles, sprained ligaments, slipped discs or even fractures of the neck. A so-called 'whiplash' injury is particularly common and occurs when the neck is suddenly flicked backwards or sideways during an awkward landing or stumble.

Symptoms: pain in the neck, usually on movement in a particular direction. This is usually accompanied by stiffness, especially the next day. If a disc has 'slipped', there may be a neuralgic pain shooting down one or other arm.

Treatment: ice in the acute phase can help to reduce inflammation. After 24 hours or so, apply gentle warmth. A surgical collar will also bring relief. When pain has subsided, gentle mobilisation exercises should be started.

Broken neck?

This is an absolutely crucial question if there is the slightest suggestion of *numbness, tingling* or *loss of function of the trunk or limbs,* associated with pain in the neck. These are symptoms of spinal cord compression. If any of these symptoms are present then a broken neck must be suspected and it is of prime importance *not to move* the casualty unless absolutely necessary for fear of increasing the pressure of the fractured vertebra on the spinal cord.

Shoulder Injuries

Again, usually the result of a fall, especially when the rider lands on the shoulder or, more often than not, on the outstretched hand. In the latter case the shoulder is wrenched, pulling muscles, tendons or ligaments, or perhaps even breaking the collar-bone.

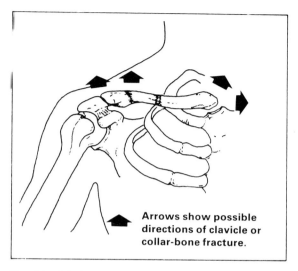

Arrows show possible directions of clavicle or collar-bone fracture.

Shoulder injuries

Symptoms: pain, bruising and limitation of movement are the main symptoms, the precise nature of which will depend on the tissue injured. Pulled muscles and tendons hurt when actively moved against resistence. Sprained ligaments also hurt on passive movement without resistance.

Treatment: as with most other acute soft-tissue injuries, initial relief can be found with a cold compress or ice-pack, immobilisation in a sling, and analgesics such as aspirin or paracetamol.

Frozen Shoulder

However, acute shoulder injuries have a nasty habit of becoming chronically and painfully stiff –

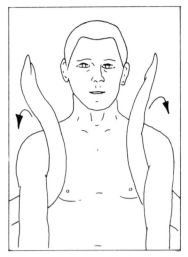
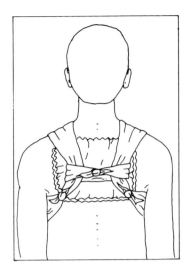
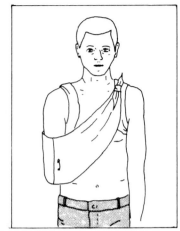

Figure-of-eight bandage (*far left and left*) and figure-of-eight bandage with forearm sling (*above*)

the so-called 'frozen shoulder'. This can be avoided by moving the shoulder passively in all directions as soon as the initial inflammation has subsided sufficiently to allow reasonably comfortable movement, i.e. usually after 24-48 hours. This passive movement should be followed a few days later by a combination of warmth and active exercise to strengthen and stabilise the shoulder.

Broken collar-bone

Usually from a fall on the forearm, elbow or the outstretched hand.

Symptoms: the diagnosis is usually obvious from the pain, bruising and deformity.

Treatment: ice and analgesics. Figure-of-eight to pull the shoulder back and bring the broken ends into alignment (*see illustration*).

Dislocated Shoulder

Another common shoulder injury caused by being thrown onto the shoulder.

Symptoms: severe pain, loss of use of the arm and deformity of the normal shoulder contour make the diagnosis obvious.

Treatment: the shoulder has to be put back by a suitably trained person, usually the doctor in the local casualty department. Thence, as per other acute shoulder injuries. (*see p. 59*)

Trunk

Severe bruising of the chest, torn chest muscles and fractured ribs can all be caused by a heavy landing, by the horse rolling onto the rider, or by being kicked or trodden upon.

Symptoms: the main symptom is of a sharp pain on movement or breathing. There is a risk that the sharp end of a broken rib might puncture the lung, causing a so-called 'sucking' injury, which is a medical emergency requiring hospitalisation.

Treatment: ice and analgesics. No strapping required. Rest for 48 hours. Then gentle breathing exercises.

Spine

Low Back Pain

Very vulnerable in a fall. Injury ranging from pulled muscles and sprained ligaments to slipped discs and fractures.

Treatment: warmth. massage, analgesics and rest on a firm mattress can all help. Sometimes manipulation is required for vertebrae that have been jolted out of alignment. It is a mistake to return to riding with residual acute low back pain. You will simply re-injure the back, and give yourself chronic lumbago.

Prevention: back and trunk exercises will help to prevent injury. It is not advisable to wear a lumbar support corset when riding; it tends to weaken the back. A back protector is a valuable protection when racing or riding across country.

Pelvis

A heavy fall on the behind can fracture the pelvis. It can also be broken when the horse rolls on to the rider.

Symptoms: what usually occurs is that one of the bones at the front of the pelvis is broken, this is accompanied by bruising and severe tenderness, while there is great difficulty in walking or bearing weight. The fracture may also damage the bladder or its outlet pipe.

Treatment: do not move the casualty unnecessarily. Send for an ambulance; urgent hospitalisation is required.

Legs

Riding Muscle Strain

This recurrent injury to the long muscle on the inside of the thigh – the adductor muscle, or its insertions commonly known as the riding muscles. These muscles play a crucial part in riding, providing the inward force of the thigh to maintain stability in the saddle. One of these muscles can be strained or pulled by a sudden or unaccustomed stretching, as can occur if the rider is dislodged sideways in the saddle, or has to grip excessively. Riding energetically after a long period out of the saddle is a recipe for straining the riding muscles.

Treatment: the pain, tenderness and, perhaps, bruising can be relieved with ice-packs, analgesics and rest.

With this, and other soft-tissue injuries, various forms of physiotherapy are practised to mobilise injured tissue and to stimulate the blood supply to assist healing. But repair is a long process and only rest from hard action will do the trick. Should a riding muscle be pulled when far from home, a bandage strapped round the top of the thigh, either under or over the breeches, will do much to ease the pain. Also shortening the stirrup leathers will help.

Knee and Ankle Injuries

These injuries can occur in falls onto the leg, or if the leg is caught under the horse when both rider and mount go down. Another cause is if the foot gets twisted sharply backwards by catching on some passing object such as a gatepost or stout branch. Bruising and sprains are the main problems. Riding boots help to protect the foot, ankle and lower leg, but tend to convey the wrenching effect to the knee. Fractures of the lower leg are not uncommon.

Treatment: soft-tissue injuries should be treated with the classic regime of R-I-C-E, i.e. rest, ice, compression and elevation (*see p. 65*). In practice this means that ice-packs or cold compresses should be applied to the bruised or swollen area as soon as possible, and the rider should rest the leg in a raised position. Firm bandaging can help to reduce the swelling and keep the injured part immobile in the first 24-48 hours. Analgesics will help to relieve the pain. When the inflammation has subsided, passive stretching movements can be started to regain full flexibility of the joints and, after a few days, active working exercises to build up strength again. If a fracture is suspected, the rider should go to hospital for X-ray and treatment.

General Ailments and Conditions

It is also useful for sportsmen and women to know something about the more general ailments and conditions that are difficult to avoid, whatever their chosen sport.

Skin and Subcutaneous Tissue

The skin and subcutaneous tissues are most vulnerable to friction and impact.

Blisters

These are caused by repeated friction of unprotected skin in which the outer layer of skin (epidermis) is separated from the inner layer (dermis) by inflammatory tissue fluid — or occasionally blood (the blood blister).

Treatment: if the blister is not likely to cause trouble it can be left alone to settle, but if in danger of being rubbed, cover it with a piece of sticking plaster.

Usually, however, it is threatening to burst and this is the moment when infection can occur. On these occasions it is best to lance it under sterile conditions. First cleanse the skin thoroughly with antiseptic. Then sterilise a needle in a flame for a few seconds and holding it parallel to the skin puncture the edge of the blister (*do not remove the loose skin*). Gently dab dry and squeeze to remove the fluid, then cover with a porous sticking plaster.

Prevention: you can prevent blisters by using sticking plaster to cover any rubbing point that is beginning to feel sore. The first indications of a blister are likely to be a soreness and reddening of the area.

Abrasions (Grazes)

Abrasions are due to the scuffing away of the epidermis completely.

Treatment: cleanse under a running tap to wash away dirt or grit (or use an antiseptic solution). When thoroughly clean, allow wound to dry, or dry by dabbing with a sterile gauze, and cover with a porous dressing.

Minor Cuts

Minor cuts should be treated similarly and covered with a sticking plaster. For more severe lacerations and bleeding see First Aid, p. 67.

Deep, Penetrating Wounds

Deep, penetrating wounds, such as caused by a nail spiking the foot, may need a tetanus injection. If the wound has been made by an object which you suspect as being infected, you are advised as a matter of course to have a precautionary tetanus injection.

Bruises (Contusions)

Bruises are areas of skin and subcutaneous tissue in which the tiny capillaries are damaged by a sudden blow. (The colouring of a bruise is due to blood oozing into the tissue.)

Treatment: an ice-pack (ice cubes in a towel – it is a mistake to apply ice direct to the skin [*see illustration*]) applied as soon as possible to the bruise will help to reduce the colouring and swelling. However, if the blow was severe, bruising may mask a fracture of the underlying bone and an X-ray is advisable.

Ice-pack

Muscle Injuries

These are usually due to repeated over-use or sudden over-stretching of untuned muscles. Most can be prevented by adequate fitness and training, and the all-important warm-up before strenuous exercise.

Muscle Aches (Muscle Soreness, Stiffness)

Muscle aches are caused by imposing unaccustomed exercise on groups of untrained muscles.

When muscles are worked hard they will swell with tissue fluid from the capillaries surrounding the muscle fibres. The fluid bathes the fibres and carries away irritant waste products of muscle contraction. *Untrained* muscles remain swollen with fluid long after exercise has stopped and this causes pain and stiffness which can take place as much as 12-24 hours afterwards, although usually much sooner.

Treatment: muscle aches can be relieved by warmth to increase the blood flow (e.g. a hot bath, shower, hot-water bottle or embrocation). Gentle massage and kneading the affected muscle may also help, especially while under hot water.

Muscle Spasm (Cramp)

Cramp is a sudden involuntary contraction of a muscle – classically the calf – causing temporary but crippling pain. It usually results from over-exertion, poor co-ordination or extreme cold – when the muscles tense – or extreme heat – when excessive sweating can lead to salt depletion.

Treatment: the most effective way to deal with cramp is to stretch the knotted muscle, in order to pull it out of spasm, and then massage it along its length.

Prevention: in hot weather add a pinch or two of salt to a fruit drink.

Stitch

A stitch is a spasm or cramp of a muscle in the side of the trunk, usually felt between or below the lower ribs.

Treatment: it can be eased by taking a deep breath in and holding it. Other techniques are to flex the trunk to the side away from the stitch or push the fingers deep into the side and bend forward.

Prevention: avoid exertion within two hours of a heavy meal.

Muscle Pulls or Tears

Muscle pulls or tears are the most common form of muscle injury and are caused by a muscle suddenly becoming over-stretched and rupturing some of the fibres. This causes intense pain, swelling and loss of function. A pulled muscle is often the result of a sudden awkward or unexpected movement in sport – a twist, or sudden stop or turn.

Treatment: stop immediately, for it is essential to rest the injured muscle as soon as possible (it would be agony to use it anyway). Apply an ice-pack and strap the pack to the injured muscle with a firm bandage in order to apply compression. If possible, elevate the injured part to help drain away inflammatory fluid.

This routine is the classic prescription for soft-tissue injuries and is sometimes given the shorthand name of R-I-C-E. (i.e. rest – ice – compression – elevation).

After 48 hours start gentle mobilisation exercises: flex the injured part back and forwards *gently*, taking care to avoid painful movement. It may also be useful to try alternate hot and cold treatments (hot towels/ice-packs alternating every 20-30 minutes). After a few days' passive stretching, you can begin active exercise, building up gradually to full activity in a few weeks.

Prevention: to avoid pulled or torn muscles it is essential to carry out a thorough warm-up before exercise (*see p. 27*).

Tendons

These are the tough fibrous strands on which muscles tug to flex or extend joints. Tendons are sometimes strained, partially torn or completely ruptured.

Symptoms: these range from pain and swelling to total loss of function.

Treatment: for lesser injuries the R-I-C-E routine (*see above*) should be started immediately; the cold compress reduces inflammation and damage. If the tendon is ruptured (and the muscles then bunch into a knot or spasm), medical attention should be sought.

Tendon Sheath

In some sports, over-use of a particular joint can lead to an irritation of the tendon sheath or lining. The resulting inflammation is called *tenosynovitis* (tendonitis) and causes shooting pain when the joint is moved.

Tendinous Insertions

Additionally, where the bulk of a muscle is anchored to a bone there are short tendinous insertions. These can sometimes be torn, usually when movement is suddenly blocked and the muscle is jarred (e.g. a squash player hitting the wall, a football player mis-kicking). The shin and elbow are classic sites of such tendinous insertions. When torn, this leads to 'shin splints' for the former and 'tennis elbow' for the latter.

Treatment: applying an ice-pack may give relief, but rest is the only cure. Your doctor may recommend other treatments and these may alleviate the symptoms temporarily, but the trouble will return unless the limb is rested because tendons are very slow to heal.

Sprains

Sprain is the term used to describe a partially torn ligament, which is a fibrous strap binding the bones of a joint together.

If a ligament tears, the joint cannot be moved without pain and soon swells. Classic sites are the ankle, the knee and the wrist.

Treatment: immediate course of action is the R-I-C-E routine. Rest is crucial; continued use of the joint will lead to chronic disability.

Bone Injuries (see First Aid, p. 71)

Hot-weather Ailments

Heat Exhaustion

Excessive sweating can lead to loss of essential water and salts. Usually, thirst provides a strong incentive to drink to replace the water, but not the salt. Salt depletion causes the victim to feel dizzy and faint, probably with a headache. It may also bring cramp (see p. 64). If salt is not replaced soon this can lead to the highly dangerous heat stroke (see First Aid, p. 71).

Prevention: add an extra pinch or two of salt to your food in hot weather before exercise.

Prickly Heat

Prickly heat is another hot-weather condition. It is caused by high humidity making the skin waterlogged, thus blocking the sweat glands and causing irritation.

Prevention: wear light, loose cotton-type clothing and try to restrict exertion to the cooler times of the day.

Sunburn

Prevention: use a suitable sunscreen to protect exposed parts.

Treatment: sunburn can be relieved with cool water or calamine lotion.

Cold-weather Ailments

Physical activity in cold weather usually keeps you warm, but the extremities — ears, nose, fingers and toes — can be affected by cold, when they will turn white and feel numb. In extreme conditions they can even become frostbitten. So wear suitable headgear, gloves and extra socks in very cold weather.

Also, in these conditions, muscles tend to tense up. So to avoid injury it is important to carry out a thorough warm-up routine before exertion (see p.27).

Prolonged exposure to severe cold, especially if soaked to the skin, can lead to the potentially fatal hypothermia.

First Aid for Sports

There are a number of common and not-so-common, sporting emergencies. This section discusses how to deal with them until medical help arrives. Most First Aid is simple practical common sense. But some techniques – in particular mouth-to-mouth respiration and cardiac massage – can really only be learned properly from a qualified instructor.

Bleeding

Severe bleeding is usually from a deep cut (laceration), torn flesh (avulsion) or penetrating wound.

Symptoms: spurting, bright-red blood indicates that an artery has been severed and the flow must be stopped *immediately*. Oozing darker blood from the veins indicates that the situation is not so urgent but the blood flow should be stopped as soon as possible.

Treatment: with both types of blood flow the treatment is essentially the same. With a clean handkerchief, or pad of absorbent material, or even your bare hands, hold together the edges of the wound and press hard to stop bleeding.

Maintaining the pressure, lay the casualty down and raise the injured part above the level of the heart, if possible. If blood seeps through the pad put another on top. *Do not release the pressure on the wound.*

Reassure the casualty and send for medical assistance, but do not leave the casualty alone for more than a minute or two, and only if you have bound the pressure pad in place.

Gaping wounds will usually need stitches. Deep wounds, especially those caused by a dirty or muddy object, may call for an anti-tetanus injection.

Nosebleed

Treatment: pinch the soft part of the nose for 10-15 minutes, or until bleeding stops. Do not swallow blood but spit it out into a cup or basin. Do not blow or pick the nose and try to avoid sneezing for the next 12 hours. An ice-pack over the nose will also prove beneficial.

Breathing Difficulty

Choking

Choking is unusual in sports, but may occur if someone inhales chewing gum or a false tooth. A blocked windpipe makes the person struggle for breath and the lips turn blue.

Treatment: get the casualty to bend forward and give him several sharp slaps between the shoulder blades to help dislodge the blockage. If this doesn't work, try the Heimlich Manoeuvre *(see illustrations)*. If you cannot clear the blockage quickly, send for urgent medical help; an emergency tracheotomy may be necessary.

Similarly, call for urgent medical help if someone is choking due to a sharp blow to the throat which has caused internal swelling of the windpipe, or if someone has a severe attack of asthma.

The recovery, or coma position

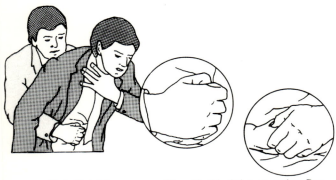

Heimlich Manoeuvre. Stand behind the casualty. Put your arm around his waist making a fist with one hand, clasping it with the other, and with thumbs resting just above his navel. Make three or four sharp pulls diagonally upwards towards you.

Stopped Breathing

If a person loses consciousness, perhaps after a blow to the head, or a faint, they may stop breathing and start to go purplish-blue. This may simply be because the tongue has fallen against the back of the throat and blocked the windpipe.

Treatment: turn the person face down so that the tongue can fall forwards. If he takes a long breath in and continues to breathe, keep him in this face down 'recovery' position (sometimes called the 'coma' position) and send for medical help (*see illustration*).

If no breath follows, then turn him face up again and start mouth-to-mouth respiration (the 'kiss of life') (*see illustrations*).

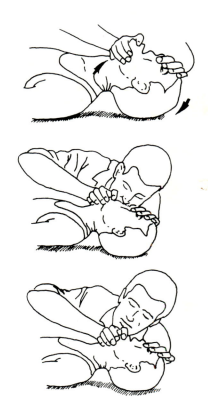

Mouth-to-mouth artificial respiration

Mouth-to-mouth Respiration: with one hand pinch his nostrils shut and push his forehead back so that his chin juts upwards. With the other hand hold his jaw open and lift it away from his neck to pull the tongue off the back of the throat. Now take a deep breath and, sealing your lips round the casualty's mouth, blow air into his lungs, watching to see his chest rise as you do so. Then remove your mouth and watch his chest fall again. Do this four times and then check the pulse (see p. 9). If the heart is beating, continue mouth-to-mouth at the rate of 16-18 breaths a minute, checking the pulse every minute or so. If you are doing the job properly the casualty's lips and tongue should become a healthy-looking pink. Keep the respiration going until help arrives or until the casualty starts to breathe spontaneously, in which case turn him face down into the recovery position (see illustration).

If you cannot feel his pulse, or he remains purple despite several good respirations, then his heart has stopped beating, and you must start cardiac massage immediately (see p. 69).

Heart Problems

Heart Attack

This is a not uncommon misfortune that may befall the unfit (usually men) who suddenly over-exert themselves. Most people survive their first heart attack, but smokers have double the risk of dying.

Symptoms: the classic symptom of a heart attack is a heavy vice-like pain in the chest — like

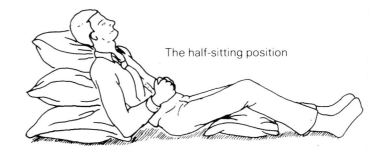
The half-sitting position

severe indigestion — which may spread to the arms or jaw. The victim usually feels faint and sick.

Treatment: if you suspect a heart attack, send someone for an ambulance, but do not leave the victim alone.

If he remains conscious, rest and reassurance are the most important things. Get him in a half-sitting position with his shoulders propped on a rolled up coat or blanket (see illustration). Loosen his clothing and cover him with a coat or towel. Do *not* give him anything by mouth, not even brandy or aspirin. Stay with him until help arrives.

If he loses consciousness and stops breathing suspect cardiac arrest (stopped heart) which calls for immediate cardiac massage, and mouth-to-mouth respiration.

Stopped Heart (Cardiac Arrest)

This is to be suspected if a person collapses unconscious and stops breathing. The victim will probably go an ashen colour with purple lips and tongue. The cause may be a heart attack or severe attack following haemorrhage or crush injury.

Treatment: feel for the casualty's pulse. Put two fingers at *one side* of his Adam's apple and press firmly. If you cannot feel pulsations, try the other side. Look at the pupils of his eyes. No pulse and wide fixed pupils spells cardiac arrest. Start cardiac massage immediately. *This is not to be attempted if the heart is beating* (*see illustrations*).

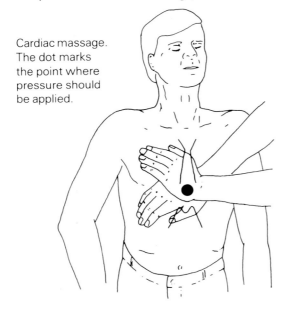

Cardiac massage. The dot marks the point where pressure should be applied.

Cardiac Massage: lay the person on his back on firm ground. Quickly clear his mouth of any vomit or blood clot with a sweep or two of your finger. Give four breaths of mouth-to-mouth respiration as above. This may be enough to stimulate the heart into action, so quickly check the heart again.

If there is still no pulse, kneel alongside the casualty. Put the heel of one hand on the lower half of his breast-bone in the midline, just above the V-shaped notch made by the ribs. Cover this hand with the heel of the other. Now keeping your arms straight, push down on your hands, moving his breastbone down about 6.25 cm (1½ in.) and release. Repeat this pressure about 80 times a minute. Count to yourself: one pressure, two pressure, three pressure . . . etc. After 15 pressures, give two more respirations, and then continue pressures. Keep going with 15 pressures, 2 respirations etc. Every few minutes stop to check the pulse. If you feel one, stop cardiac massage but continue respirations. If spontaneous breathing starts, put him in the recovery position (*see illustration*). Do not abandon your efforts until help arrives.

Unconsciousness

Usually caused by a blow to the head, but sometimes due to a diabetic coma, epileptic fit or heart attack (*see above*).

The most important action is to check for breathing. If the casualty is not breathing, mouth-to-mouth respiration must be started immediately.

If the casualty is unconscious but still breathing, turn him face down into the 'recovery' or 'coma' position (*see p. 69*). This allows the tongue to fall forwards away from the back of the throat where it would block the windpipe.

Send for immediate medical help, but do not leave the casualty unattended, check his breathing every few minutes.

Head Injury

This can range from a cut scalp to a fractured skull, but usually refers to a blow on the head sufficient to knock out the victim for seconds or minutes.

Concussion

The likely consequence is concussion, a temporary disorientation causd by jarring the brain.This may be accompanied by giddiness and memory loss.

Contusion (Bruising)

More serious is brain contusion, which leaves a scar in the brain substance and usually causes some permanent loss of memory and intellectual capacity (i.e. 'punch-drunk').

Compression

The most serious and life-threatening result is compression: an inter-cranial haemorrhage (bleeding inside the skull). The build-up of pressure can rapidly lead to loss of consciousness and death, unless the pressure is released by emergency surgery. Compression can occur up to 48 hours after injury.

Symptoms: drowsiness, confusion, dilation of one or both pupils of the eye.

Treatment: any person knocked out by a head injury should be made to lie quietly and be looked at every half hour or so to check the level of consciousness.

If you observe any of the symptoms of compression listed above, get the victim to hospital immediately.

Facial Injury

Black Eye

Usually looks far worse than it is. As soon as you can, apply an ice-pack or cold compress to prevent or reduce the swelling. It is wise to have the eye checked by a doctor to make sure that vision is not impared.

Broken Nose

Usually accompanied by bleeding, swelling and deformed appearance. Bleeding should be stopped as described above (*p. 67*). Sometimes the nose can be straightened immediately, but usually it is best to put on an ice-pack or cold compress and get the casualty to hospital.

Broken cheekbones and broken jaws should also be covered with an ice-pack to reduce swelling and the casualty taken to hospital.

Fractures and Dislocations

Broken bones and disrupted joints are usually obvious, especially in the more serious cases. Sometimes, however, swelling and bruising can mask such injuries, e.g. stress fracture of the foot.

Treatment: it is important not to try to bear weight on a fracture or dislocation as this could damage a nerve or blood vessel. It is also important not to try to straighten the injury, unless you know precisely what you are doing, for you could cause even more damage.

The most useful thing to do is to keep the injured part as immobile as possible – use splints, slings or stretchers as necessary. The casualty should be taken to hospital where the injury can be X-rayed and the deformity reduced under medical supervision, with an anaesthetic if necessary.

Environmental Emergencies

Heat Stroke

This is a very serious condition and can occur after prolonged exertion in a very hot or humid environment. It is caused by the body's temperature-regulating system breaking down and, as a result, the temperature rises alarmingly.

Symptoms: the victim has a hot dry skin, rapid pulse and looks flushed. Confusion and coma can follow rapidly.

Treatment: *medical attention is urgent.* The important thing is to *cool* the victim down as quickly as possible with water or ice, and then to keep him fanned to induce cooling.

Frostbite

This is also potentially serious. The body is composed of 70 per cent water and if ice-crystals form in human tissue it is destroyed.

Treatment: numbed and frozen extremities should be got into the warm as soon as possible and held against warm skin. *Do not apply direct heat and do not rub the frozen part* – you might literally rub the flesh away. Do not stand or walk on frozen toes or feet, but rest with the feet up.

Index

After-exercise Care 47
Aids 35
Avoiding Injury 41
Azoturia 51

Back Protector 43
Balance 33
Biting Flies 52
Bitting 43
Boots 42
Breeches 43
Bringing a Horse to Peak Fitness 46

Clipping 48
Clothing 42-3
Colic 51
Confidence 33
Corns 53

Dental Care 52
Development Work 46
Dressage 39

Endurance Riding 38
Exercise Circuits for Riding 40
External Parasites 52

Falling 42
Fast Work 47
Feeding 53
Fitness Needs of Riding 39-41

Galloping 47
Gloves 43
Grooming 48

Hands 36
Hats 42
Hoof Care 53
Horse Fitness Indicators 49-50
    Body Heat 50
    Breathing 49
    Dung 50
    Gut Noises 50
    Head 49
    Injuries 50
    Skin 49
    Urine 50
Horse, Natural Fitness of 45
Hunting 38

Influenza 52

Keeping Your Horse Fit and Healthy

Lameness 50
Leathers 43
Levels of Riding Fitness 37-39
Lice 52
Limbering Up 41
Long-distance Riding 38

Mental Attitude 41

Mites 52

Paces 36
Paddocks 53
Preliminary Work 46
Preventative Medicine 52-4
Pus in Foot 53

Rhinopnewmonitis 52
Riding, General Fitness
    Requirements of 33
Riding Position 34

Saddles 43
Schooling 39
Stables 53
Stamina Exercises for Riding 39
Stirrups 43
Stock 43
Strength Exercises for Riding 40
Suppleness Exercises for Riding 40

Tack 43-4
Taking a Horse's Pulse 50
Teeth 52
Tetanus 52
Ticks 52

Worming 52